Holy Wars:

Root Causes

Dr. Thomas Moore

Holy Wars: Root Causes

Published by VIP Ink Publishing

Cover Layout and Editing By Whyte Lady Designs L.L.C.
Graphic Design by Sarah McClain

www.vipinkpublishing.com

ISBN 13: 978-1-939670-02-1
ISBN: 1-939670-02-1

Printed in the USA.

Table of Contents

About Dr. Thomas Moore

Dr. Thomas Moore is a Christian Psychologist and Psychotherapist and is best known for his work in the world of spiritual warfare. He has written a series of seven books entitled Holy Wars. Look for these other titles by Dr. Thomas Moore coming soon to a book store near you:

Holy Wars: Myths

Holy Wars: Root Causes

Holy Wars: Breaking Curses

Holy Wars: Power In The Blood

Holy Wars: Bible-Based Principles

Holy Wars: Breaking Occult Spells

Holy Wars: The Battle Is The Lord's

Introduction:

Breaking Spiritual Strongholds

<u>Healing The Wounded Spirit And Dealing With Root Causes</u>

This book on deliverance and healing exclusively covers spiritual areas. Spiritual areas are distinct from social, physical, and material areas. Spiritual areas encompass matters experienced in the unseen spiritual realm of the mind, emotions and will. The matters experienced in the unseen realm cannot be observed by any of us whether in a counseling situation, as an intercessor, as a patient, or as mere listener. The only thing that can be observed in the seen realm is the behavior resulting from the spiritual problem. The behavior is not the problem itself. It is only a symptom or a sign of the actual problem. The spiritual areas of the mind, emotions and will are referred to as mental health areas in the secular world. They have separated unseen mental health concerns from observable physical health concerns.

From a biblical perspective the field of mental health is primarily a spiritual health sphere. What the secular world calls mental health is referred to as spiritual health in Christianity. Christian spiritual health encompasses not just mental health, but also emotional health, and the health of the will (inner drive, passion, zeal, self-control). It this spiritual nature of our inner makeup that the secular world finds itself limited to dealing with. Healing the wounded spirit is not just a cognitive, mental or brain chemistry issue. It is beyond that. It is a spiritual matter.

The primary source in the deliverance and healing process is the Holy Spirit. He is the healer of any wounded spirit or any spiritual wounds we may have. It is deep calling unto deep, the human spirit calling unto the Holy Spirit. Spiritual health is thus a spirit calling unto Spirit being. The Holy Spirit's key requirements from us are

1) that we do our part and
2) that we cooperate with him in his deliverance and healing work.

Spiritual health is more essential than any other area of our lives. It is more important than our physical health, physical looks, social health, and our material health (wealth). The bible says, "A man's spirit sustains him in sickness, but a crushed spirit who can bear?" Proverbs 18:14. The human spirit is the engine of a person's life. It is a person's true makeup while his/her body enables the spirit to express itself on earth. The body, under the influence of the spirit, interacts with the physical realm. The spirit rules the body. Our physical bodies in their different makeup of looks, race, gender, genetics and other features are insignificant compared to the importance of our spiritual makeup.

Both spiritual strongholds and healing the wounded spirit are intertwined and are dealt with in the same way. This book lays the principles for the Holy Spirit's healing work. It outlines the areas of our input and how these facilitate the inner healing work of the Holy Spirit. It digs deeper into dealing with the root causes or doorways of spiritual problems that linger in our unseen spiritual makeup. Deliverance and healing comes through dealing with the root causes or doorways of entry for spiritual wounds.

Our spiritual makeup is our treasure deserving all the care far above our physical makeup. It determines our outcomes not only in this life, but in the life to come when Christ returns. It is hoped that this book meets its goal in equipping you and those you serve with effective spiritual health principles. It is a book appropriate for everyone in the body of Christ.

Chapter 1:

Our Triune Nature: Spirit, Soul and Body

Our make up as humans is triune

We exist in three in parts – spirit, soul and body. The spirit part of us is what relates with the soul which in turn relates with the body. We are made in God's image in our spiritual makeup. Our physical bodies are only for the purpose of physical dealings on this physical earth. We know more about our physical bodies than we do about our spiritual bodies. This book sheds some light on the nature of our spiritual makeup, how to maintain its wellbeing, and receiving God's healing whenever there is injury to the spirit.

We are spirits living in bodies

The real person in us is not our bodies. It is our inner makeup of the soul and the spirit. We are therefore spirits living in bodies and not the other way around. Our bodies are not our true selves but the spirit of each of us is. Thank God that it is not our bodies that are made in God's image. They are made for our spirits to express themselves on earth. We'd have a never-ending debate if our bodies were made in God's image. We'd be debating about his gender, his race, genetics, height, weight, age, looks etc.

Each of us has one spirit, just as we each have one body. This spirit is largely referred to as the human spirit. This serves to distinguish it from other spirits, such as God's angels (which are also spirits) and fallen angels (which are spirits too). It also distinguishes it from the Holy Spirit.

We each have a physical body for use in the physical realm

The physical body is what relates with the rest of the world. The physical body is for using in the physical earthly realm. Without our bodies our assignments on earth end. The earth is only for people with physical bodies. That is why the dead cannot relate with us who are still alive and they cannot relate with the physical realm. Some claim the dead can relate with us.

Once the physical body dies the spirit in each of us leaves the body and awaits its destination –heaven or hell. It means our usefulness as spirits on earth has ended. The body goes back to its earthly domain by decomposing. There is no point in contributing to ending our usefulness prematurely by being careless with physiological nutritional and health needs of the body.

Myles Munroe while being interviewed by Benny Hinn on his book Understanding the Purpose and Power of Prayer: Earthly License for Heavenly Interference said, "Any spirit on earth without a body is illegal…The reason why humans can cast demons out is that the humans do have a body. It's the body that makes the humans authoritatively legal on earth." Benny Hinn interrupted, "That is why demons seek a body to regain their dominion."

Munroe continued, "You just stole my next point… Every spirit is trying to find a body. Can I give you another shocker? Even the Holy Spirit. Because He cannot function here without a body. That's why we're called the body of Christ. And it says our bodies are temples of the Holy Spirit, because He Himself needs to be legally here in order to function."

"Your most important asset on earth is not your spirit. It's your body. Because without your body your spirit also becomes illegal. That's why when you die you have to leave…Every spirit needs a body to be legal on earth because of God's law (giving humans with bodies dominion over the earth)…That is why God put so much value on your body physically that he provided healing to make it last long (on earth)," (Myles Munroe, on This is Your Day, Sky Angel Satellite TV, July 13, 2004).

This is all to supplement our understanding of the importance our physical bodies have. With an appropriate perspective on their importance we can cease feeling guilty when caring for them. Munroe did exaggerate by saying *"Your most important asset on earth is not your spirit. It's your body."* What use is the body without a healthy spirit? So it's our soul and spirit that's most important even while here on earth.

However, when seen from the point he was trying to make we cannot blame him. He was trying to say that for the spirit of each of us to have any existence and use on earth it needs a body. *"It's the body that makes the humans authoritatively legal on earth."* The body is essential for our existence on earth. Teilihard de Chardin (1881-1955), a Jesuit priest said, *"We are not human beings having a spiritual experience, but spiritual beings having a human experience."* He is also quoted to have said, *"You are not a human being in search of a spiritual experience. You are a spiritual being immersed in a human experience."*

In order to continue having this human experience we need to remain in our bodies for as long as the Lord wills; not for as long as we carelessly stretch the tolerance of our bodies. They are precious vessels for our assignments on earth. God is so interested in our human experience that even God's angels are surprised why God makes it such a big deal. We cannot afford to minimize our worth to God through our existence in these physical suites called bodies. Through these bodies we can accomplish so much for God's glory on earth. That's why the angels marvel at us.

"What is man, that thou art mindful of him? and the son of man, that thou visitest him? For thou hast made him a little lower than the angels, and hast crowned him with glory and honor. Thou maddest him to have dominion over the works of thy hands; thou hast put all things under his feet: All sheep and oxen, yea, and the beasts of the field; The fowl of the air, and the fish of the sea, and whatsoever passeth through the paths of the seas," Psalm 8:4-8 God made us rulers or to have dominion over the works of his hands on earth. Even over the salvation of fellow humanity he is counting on us. He works through us, in the body of Christ, to reach the lost; not independently of us.

"How can they believe in the one of whom they have not heard? And how can they hear without someone preaching to them? As it is written, 'How beautiful are the feet of those who bring good news!'" Romans 10:14. Our existence here on earth is important not primarily for our own sake but primarily for the sake of others; the lost and fellow believers in the body of Christ. We have a divine responsibility to ensure we're treating the temples of the Holy Spirit well so that he can effectively do his work in reaching others.

This book is concerned with the well being of the spirit. The spirit is the engine of the body. Without a healthy spirit the physical body is of no use, no matter how beautiful and healthy it may be. So it's worth knowing how to care for the spirit far more than it is to care for the physical body.

We each have a soul to connect the spirit with the body

The soul is what connects the intricate parts of the spirit in order to use the body while on earth. It is the middleperson between the spirit and the body. The soul therefore serves to connect the two parts together: the invisible (the spirit) and the visible (the body). It consists of the mind, will and emotional faculties.

However the spirit and the soul are not as easily divisible as we assume. The soul which connects with the spirit is sometimes referred to interchangeably with the spirit in the bible. This is because the spirit and the soul are not as easily divisible as we understand them. Our understanding of them is only at their simplest level. The bible only gives us a generalized picture of our spiritual makeup. In eternity we will know more about our unseen makeup.

In this book we will consider the soul and the spirit as one and the same. This will make it easier to focus on the essentials while still being totally consistent with scripture. We will refer to the mind, will and emotional faculties as being part of the spirit as much as they are part of the soul.

There is a book I'd recommend for in-depth biblical analysis on the spirit, soul and body. It is a book titled "*Free Indeed: Fullness for the Whole Man, Spirit, Soul and Body*" by Tom Marshall. It's a worthy read if you can find it among online stores. The last time I checked (Dec. 2007) it was out of print.

Tom Marshall (1921-1993), a missionary in New Zealand, went to be with Lord in 1993. His books are still treasured today. You can still be able to purchase low-priced used copies at Amazon.com. AllBookstores.com, a book price comparison website, also shows all the major online bookstores where the book can be found. Some local Christian bookstores may also have it. I bought mine in Nairobi, Kenya.

In "*Free Indeed: Fullness for the Whole Man, Spirit, Soul and Body*", Marshall goes to great lengths in biblically distinguishing our triune makeup of spirit, soul and body. I consider this book a Christian classic, published in 1975. It will supplement Christian principles on healing the wounded spirit that this book may not have covered.

Chapter 2:

Spiritual Strongholds in the Mind, Emotions & Will

Passage in the bible on spiritual strongholds

There is one important passage in the bible that uses the word "strongholds" in reference to spiritual battles we face. Other passages that use the word "strongholds" are in the Old Testament and have no parallels to the following passage.

"The weapons we fight with are not the weapons of the world. On the contrary, they have divine power to demolish **strongholds**. We demolish arguments and every pretension that sets itself up against the knowledge of God, and we take captive every thought to make it obedient to Christ. And we will be ready to punish every act of disobedience, once your obedience is complete," 2 Corinthians 10:4-6.

Some misunderstanding on tearing down strongholds

There is a misunderstanding among some in the body of Christ on tearing down spiritual strongholds. This is worth addressing since it has led some believers to be preoccupied with directly confronting evil spirits.

It has been erroneously assumed that tearing down strongholds is going after evil spirits and pulling them down in geographical regions, in the heavens, in circumstances, etc. This interpretation takes the passage completely out of context.

No scripture even advocates direct confrontation with Satan as a way of punishing his acts of disobedience among people or matters in our lives. Yet there are plenty of scriptures showing that our prayers to God combined with our obedience to him accomplish the impossible. It's astonishing how powerful prayer is.

On directly confronting spirits, G. Richard Fisher says, "Biblically taking cities for God by crippling and disarming the demons of the city is nowhere taught in Scripture. Paul preached the Gospel in each city without dramatics or evasive claims. We do not find Paul doing "prayer walks" and spiritual stakeouts. Logic tells us that for all the time the "demon busters" have been at it, they should have had these cities all under control by now and demon free.

In the new theatrics of demon busting, one word, "stronghold," has been taken out of 2 Corinthians 10 and used to create an entire theology. The context of chapter 10 is confronting false belief. If anyone is tearing down strongholds, it is the counter cult and apologetic movement (the counter cult and apologetic movement are the people that expose false teachings in and outside the body of Christ). Dualistic demonism is in itself a stronghold of error and false teaching," (G. Richard Fisher, "Walking in the Shadow of the Walk").

What are spiritual strongholds from a biblical perspective?

"The weapons we fight with are not the weapons of the world. On the contrary, they have divine power to demolish strongholds. We demolish arguments and every pretension that sets itself up against the knowledge of God, and we take captive every thought to make it obedient to Christ. And we will be ready to punish every act of disobedience, once your obedience is complete," 2 Corinthians 10:4-6. In the New International Version (NIV) bible this passage is in a chapter titled "*Paul's Defense of His Ministry.*"

Paul maintains that we're not to live by the standards of this world. He said we should not be like "some people who think that we live by the standards of this world." These were among believers. Some people were stirring up believers against him.

"Matthew Henry Complete Commentary on the Whole Bible" notes that, "There was no place in which the apostle Paul met with more opposition from false apostles than at Corinth; he had many enemies there…Though he was so blameless and inoffensive in all his carriage."

Paul was therefore referring to punishing "every act of disobedience" among believers who were not walking right with God. The passage does not imply punishing the disobedience of Satan by directly confronting him. It meant confronting the disobedience among believers. This disobedience would be punished not by weapons of this world (such as arguments, lawsuits, physical confrontation or war) but by our spiritual weapons that "have divine power to demolish strongholds" (such as prayer, fasting, walking in love, God's word and faith).

Spiritual strongholds are strongly established sinful ways, false beliefs, and behaviors that have gained a strong influence over a person to the extent that each stronghold "sets itself up against the knowledge of God". In areas that the strongholds are established, an individual is either unable to consistently follow God's word or is unable to accept it because these spiritual strongholds have an excessive influence on him. Strongholds are high levels of demonic influence, not possession, in any area of the spiritual faculties of an individual. Our spiritual faculties consist of our minds, our emotions and our will power. Think of people caught up in some sinful behavior like atheism, unbelief, stealing, greed, alcohol addiction, drugs, sexual sins, promiscuity, pornography, homosexuality, uncontrollable anger (temper tantrums), compulsive gambling etc. They feel easily pulled to or controlled by whatever matter that is entrenched into their lifestyle.

Strongholds can be divinely demolished through our indirect weapons of spiritual warfare and deliverance. They are not demolished by directly confronting certain assumed spirits in geographical territories, familiar spirits, generational spirits, Jezebel spirits, spirits of division, spirits of unforgiveness, spirits of addiction, or any other spirits of this and that.

Paul says with our spiritual weapons (that are indirect in nature) we're able to "demolish arguments and every pretension that sets itself up against the knowledge of God, and we take captive every thought to make it obedient to Christ". He then says our obedience to God enables us to "punish every act of disobedience, once your (our) obedience (to God) is complete".

One way that our obedience to God has punishing effects on the works of Satan on earth is through prayer. Our obedient lives are weapons of righteousness that enable our prayers not to be hindered. This is indirect spiritual warfare. No direct confrontation with Satan or his evil spirits is required.

<u>Two types of strongholds: known and unknown (hidden)</u>

The passage on strongholds was actually made in reference to believers, not to unbelievers. This does not mean unbelievers have no strongholds! It's worse for them in a spiritual sense, as the bible says, "The god of this age has blinded the minds of unbelievers, so that they cannot see the light of the gospel of the glory of Christ," 2 Corinthians 4:4.

Thus our outreach to unbelievers is centered on removing the most serious spiritual stronghold, which is the spiritual veil that covers them from seeing the salvation gospel. The veil remover is not us. It's God by the power of his Holy Spirit (himself). We proclaim the gospel and the Holy Spirit goes into the minds of people to open them up to receiving the salvation gospel.

In our own lives as believers we've our own veils to remove. These veils constitute strongholds that hinder us from living true Christian lives. Spiritual strongholds are in two types:

1) **Known and easily discernible strongholds: Operating as known sins** - The obvious strongholds include matters that the bible clearly forbids and matters that are culturally unacceptable. Even though a person may know they're forbidden and unacceptable he/she may still proceed to carry them out time and again. The repetition nature of such matters is what shows that strongholds have been established in an area(s) of concern.

2) **Unknown and hidden strongholds: Operating under ignorance** - These are strongholds we're not even aware that they exist. They include matters we lack understanding in, matters that the bible imprecisely forbids, and some matters that are culturally acceptable but are biblically unacceptable. Unknown, obscure or hidden strongholds operate under the veil of ignorance.

It is likely that the false apostles who were opposing Apostle Paul by trying to teach another gospel version were doing it out of ignorance. Paul was aware that their strongholds were operating through their ignorance to the true gospel.

The false apostles opposing him gave him a hard time at Corinth. They spread a bad report that he was a false apostle who was not worth associating with. In actual fact they were the ones that were the real false apostles. They were trying to preach worldliness among believers. They were undermining the call not to live by the standards of this world. In his teachings Paul emphasized that believers should not be like "some people who think that we live by the standards of this world". Their lack of understanding on the scriptures made them easy vessels to be under the influence of evil spirits that spread false teachings. They could not even see it that they had strongholds of demonic influence causing them to resist the true gospel.

Strong resistance to the truth is one major characteristic of being under strongholds working through ignorance. A person under such strongholds does not even bother to go and objectively compare the different points being shared. He easily resorts to opposing any other point of view out of his own flesh, not out of the spirit of love and a sound mind (understanding, objective analysis, and humility). He almost has a military-style of loyalty to points of view he embraces or points of view of his affiliated church.

This blind and military-style type of loyalty is of the flesh. It breeds and thrives on ignorance. The more ignorant a person is on a particular matter the more likely he is able to have strongholds that operate through such ignorance. It is common that our own cultures in all the different places we live in play an important role in establishing blind and military-style types of loyalty to matters we believe in.

For example, when I came to USA there were some cultural strongholds that I never knew operated in my life. Being in such a different cultural environment has been a great blessing in comparing the different cultural perspectives. It brought the opportunity to objectively look at the scriptures and to see which of the different cultural versions are more in line with the scriptures.

USA wins on some of the cultural versions while Africa and other developing regions win on others. At all costs it's worth striving to pursue whatever cultural perspective is in line with the scriptures and not to blindly embrace that which is more convenient or popular. This is not a competition. It's just giving examples on being relatively free from false beliefs on certain matters. Listed next are two examples on different regions having a better cultural version

USA & false beliefs on women's rights, a "known" stronghold

For example, USA wins on women's civil rights. Women's rights matters in Africa and other developing regions are currently centuries behind. Developing regions have their socio-economic obstacles that facilitate this vicious cycle: inadequate higher education opportunities (colleges and universities), high unemployment rates, low per capita incomes, highly patriarchal cultures, etc. These are some of the obstacles that continue to hinder progress on women's civil rights in Africa and other developing regions. They only serve to perpetuate the subordination of women in all key spheres of life.

However, they do not constitute the biggest obstacle. Solving them will not automatically improve the treatment, behavior, attitude, and perceptions of men towards women. Saudi Arabia currently has a high per capita income and can afford to empower women yet its treatment of women is one of the lowest in the world.

The root of the problem to addressing women's civil rights is at the spiritual level. The spiritual level in reference to is our spiritual faculties of our minds, our emotions and our will power. Just as the civil rights of African Americans never improved with America's economic progress until they were addressed on a spiritual level the same applies to women's rights.

In the 1960's Dr. Martin Luther King Jr. challenged the treatment, behavior, attitude, and perceptions of white people towards African Americans. His message and approach was so convincing that a majority of whites joined his call. He successfully was able to pull down strongholds of false beliefs and behaviors among people that ended up embracing his call.

By the way, among this majority of whites few of them were Christians. This is because most of the Christian whites were being fed by their pastors the message to oppose the civil rights cry. An era when Christianity could have triumphed as the champion on human rights was missed. Instead we (as Christians) ran to our strongholds of false beliefs and behaviors that gained strong influence over us for centuries on racial issues.

To this day the 1960's civil rights movement stands as a shame to Christianity for refusing to embrace equal rights on the basis of race. God was probably shaking his head as white Christians failed to objectively look at their old beliefs that were being challenged. Martin Luther King Jr., the leading figure was a devout Christian and so were most of disenfranchised African Americans. It still didn't click that God was up to something. Such resistance to change is sometimes referred to as a stiff neck behavior in the bible. Apostle Paul would have called it strongholds.

As Christians we've a bitter lesson to learn about being blindly and stubbornly defensive over every opposing viewpoint without giving it the needed biblical objective analysis. Women's civil rights matters need a fervent and clear biblical objective analysis. We cannot afford bringing up defenses with out-of-context scriptures to justify our perspectives. This civil rights matter needs all our humility, prayerfulness, in-depth biblical contextual analysis and objectivity if any strongholds are to be overcome.

The women's rights movement has been hijacked by secret occult groups who equate abortion to women's rights. This does not mean we withdraw from any participation. It means we present our Christian version, grounded in the bible, and pray that God uses it to overcome those who're using this matter for wrong reasons.

For any reader in USA the abortion topic may bring some association with political parties. The Republicans oppose abortion while the Democrats support it. However, this is only for political gain on both sides. It doesn't take much analysis to see it, nor any study of political science. It's also paradoxical that abortions increase when Republicans are in office and decrease when Democrats are in office. It's not a Republican or Democratic Party cause. It's an economic cause.

When Republicans are in office assistance to economic welfare programs that help the needy are drastically cut. With little or no support some people in poor communities resort to abortions when faced with pregnancies. This explains the increase in abortions when Republicans are in office. It shows that people primarily seek abortions for economic reasons. Thus a political party that says it opposes abortions but does not address the underlying causes is contradicting itself. It is hypocrisy. And many Christians buy this hypocrisy by aligning themselves with political parties based on what they say, and not what they do.

The decrease in abortions when Democrats are in office is also explained by their increased welfare support programs to people in poor communities. What the Democrats say in their support of abortion is not good. However what they do in increasing welfare programs to people in poor communities is commendable. It's not the best way since they give fish while ignoring the more important objective of teaching people to catch fish. However, it's still better than no fish at all and no help to learn how to fish.

The two political party illustrations were given to show that the abortion is merely a political vote grabbing issue when it's brought up; For Republicans, opposing abortion suites with their target group of voters (conservatives and Christians) and for Democrats embracing it also suites with their target group of voters (liberals and left-wing leaning people).

I'm therefore not trying to support one political party as being better than another. They're both secular institutions that do not have our true Christian agenda at heart. If they did they would have addressed the spiritual and economic reasons behind many matters plaguing the poor. The problems include higher crime rates, use and selling of illegal drugs, higher abortion rates, lawlessness, etc.

Instead their efforts and lack of effort serve to continue the status quo of ensuring an underclass exists for cheap labor and easier control. For Democrats the constant giving of fish in the long run increases dependency, breeds laziness, decreases industriousness, and lessens personal responsibility for actions. As a result people under such support hardly ever rise above their obstacles. For Republicans the lack of support to people in poor communities serves the same purpose of ensuring an underclass exists.

In my other book on breaking occult spells I cover on how some groups in the occult world have infiltrated nearly every segment in society to insure their satanic agenda reigns in this world. They've infiltrated politics, big business, the health industry and the women's rights movement. They're using the women's rights movement for population control purposes, to undermine family values, for blood rituals on aborted children, etc.

Thus it's not worth retreating to our strongholds of false beliefs and behaviors just to feel safe on the women's rights movement. We ought to participate in the women's rights movement to ensure God's agenda reigns and not the agenda of those in the occult. We ought not to sit by and allow them to use it for political gain, for abortion reasons, population control, and undermining family values.

Africa & modesty values, an "unknown" or "hidden" stronghold

An area where USA loses and could learn a lesson from Africa and other developing regions regards modesty values. To reiterate this is not a competition. It's just to give examples on being relatively free from false beliefs on certain matters. A consumerism and materialism culture has been eroding basic values on being satisfied with the simple things in life: spirituality, family, community, charity, nature, and good health. People have placed a high security in money and things at a heavy cost of sacrificing spiritual pursuits, family values, and other simple things in life.

The consumerism and materialism culture is a product of the major media players getting into a close partnership with the business world that advertise their products in the media. Promotion of consumerism makes the material "bling bling" being advertised to a specific group a part of their identity.

To feel more recognized in one's group it becomes so important to have a good amount of the products and services being advertised. To many it's more painful to feel like a social outcast in their culture and sub-culture than in questioning what's being thrown at them by the media.

There's an interesting "Happy Fathers Day" quotation circulating online. It says volumes on what consumerism has done:

- In 1900, if a father put a roof over his family's head, he was a success. Today, it takes a roof, deck, pool, and 4-car garage. And that's just the vacation home
- In 1900, fathers passed on clothing to their sons. Today, kids wouldn't touch Dad's clothes if they were sliding naked down an icicle.

- In 1900, fathers and sons would have heart-to-heart conversations while fishing in a stream. Today, fathers pluck the headphones off their sons' ears and shout, "WHEN YOU HAVE A MINUTE..."
- In 1900, a father gave a pencil box for Christmas, and the kid was all smiles. Today, a father spends $800 at Toys 'R' Us, and the kid screams: "I wanted X-Box!"
- In 1900, a happy meal was when Father shared funny stories around the table. Today, a happy meal is what Dad buys at McDonald's.
- In 1900, when fathers entered the room, children often rose to attention. Today, kids glance up and grunt, "Dad, you're invading my space."

Even some churches have picked up this false message of seek first material "bling bling" and serve God primarily by giving your offering. It may not be bluntly said this way but their obsession with money and wealth says it loud and clear. In my other book on breaking occult spells I cover on how some groups in the occult world have infiltrated the body of Christ to sow in their deceptive doctrines.

Obsession with money and wealth is not part of our Christian calling. People who want to really serve God are broken for the matters that the Holy Spirit is leading them to focus on. They're spiritually in tune with God's leading. They're willing to deny their desires of the flesh and to deny self-serving interests.

On the other hand, people who want God to serve them are preoccupied with what God can do for them. They're spiritually out of tune with God's leading and are more in tune with the flesh. They're not willing to deny their desires of the flesh and self-serving interests. The prosperity gospel is a "serve me God gospel," licensing worldliness.

The bible says, "Set your minds on things above, not on earthly things. For you died and your life is now hidden with Christ in God" Colossians 3: 2-3. Setting our minds on things above demands forsaking things below; it cannot be done by embracing both. Materialism, that is the belief system that glorifies wealth and other tangible objects above intangible and spiritual "objects", has been around as far back as written and oral history goes. The only difference now is that it has reached chronic levels. It has become a major societal disease that is worth eradicating before it eradicates society. Unfortunately this disease is already eradicating it with increased pollution, decreased social values, immorality, and decreased spirituality.

Above all materialism is the major motive that's driving the leaders of this world in pursuit of the one world government where they control all the world's resources under one roof. The false power that wealth gives will eventually lead to the battle of Armageddon as factions among leaders of this world struggle for ownership of the world's key resources. Thus materialism is what will end this world, with the battle of Armageddon being the last and most devastating war before Christ returns to save his elect.

"For the love of money is a root of all kinds of evil," 1 Timothy 6:10. The love, not the mere possession of money, is a root of all kinds of evil. Remove the word love and money ceases to have a high value and affection it gets when it's loved. People can be content with or without it. When love is removed money becomes like anything any of us have no affection to.

For example, I can live without a television. If ever I switch one on it would be for the Christian channels, news, or to watch a documentary. Getting rid of it would not reduce any amount of contentment in my life. It's just a tool and its use does not make me attached to it.

What is this love of money that the bible talks about? It's the same definition found in dictionaries. You'll easily see that the prosperity gospel falls into this category of loving money. Here's a dictionary definition of love: *A strong positive emotion of regard and affection. Passion (any object of warm affection or devotion). Enjoy (get pleasure from).* (WordNet 3.0 © Princeton University, "love").

Thus materialism does not refer to having a good career, good education, well paying job or modest material conveniences. Rather it refers to a person building his/her life around any of these earthly prizes. A person may strongly deny that he's not a materialist but his actions expose him.

His self-worth, goals and ambitions, inner desire for validation from other people, perception on security in life, satisfaction, happiness, and perception of God's blessings, all evolve around acquiring more money and earthly things. He may be in denial about worshiping the false god called money but in reality he's under the spell of this false god. Unfortunately this person is not some unbeliever but it's one among us following the prosperity gospel.

This prosperity gospel says, "Made in USA," but it has now spread worldwide like a wildfire. There's a joke in Kenya that if your business fails just become a prosperity preacher. You'll easily gather your own flock that will be willing to embrace the "give to get rich" gospel. While doing graduate studies in Kenya I actually ended up in one of these prosperity churches. The materialism gospel was well-matched with my business degree program. Going to church was like going for extra business classes on how to be super wealthy, this time using the bible. It was sweet, until by God's grace the Lord showed all the poison hiding behind this false gospel. Thus if there's anyone familiar with this materialistic gospel I'm one of them.

Christians preaching this gospel are like the Pharisees whom

Jesus called *"blind guides" Matthew 15:14*. It is thus the blind leading the blind. The blind give innocent Christians the worldly concept of money that has nothing to do with Christianity. These blind guides are experts at twisting the scriptures. To such God says, *"You say, 'I am rich; I have acquired wealth and do not need a thing.' But you do not realize that you are wretched, pitiful, poor, blind and naked," Revelation 3:17*.

As a result worldliness is given a welcome seat in Christianity. Christians compromise their spiritual pursuits, walking in purity, passion for the lost and needy etc., by making the acquisition of wealth their primary goal. Some may assume they're not doing so but when anyone is willing to look with an open mind at the opposing biblical perspectives it's likely he/she will realize it. A biblical reality check says glorifying earthly riches is not our Christian agenda.

One person in prominent circles who received a biblical reality check is Jim Bakker. He was once a well known prosperity American televangelist. He apologized after realizing the emptiness of this false gospel. *"For years, I helped propagate an impostor, not a true gospel, but another gospel,"* Bakker wrote in his 1996 book titled, *"I Was Wrong"*. How did Bakker realize he was teaching an erroneous doctrine? It was by his first time of reading the Bible all the way when he was in prison for defrauding Heritage USA investors. May none of us receive our wake-up moment on certain false teachings through regrettable moments, may we seek the truth and apply it without learning it through the hard way.

Bakker wrote in his book, "The more I studied the Bible; however, I had to admit that the prosperity message did not line up with the tenor of Scripture. My heart was crushed to think that I led so many people astray. I was appalled that I could have been so wrong, and I was deeply grateful that God had not struck me dead as a false prophet." Jim Bakker, "I Was Wrong" Nashville,

TN: Thomas Nelson, 1996.

Christians blindly caught up in this false gospel are not going to hell if they're innocently deceived. They're part of the body of Christ, like any of us. However this does not justify the false teachings. They're to be addressed and the bible clearly shows that they're false teachings. False teachings are not justifiable, whether on women's rights, money, or spiritual warfare.

Summary on the two types of strongholds

This section has covered on the two types of strongholds: known and unknown (hidden) strongholds. The examples given are a tiny fraction of hidden strongholds lurking among us, around us, in the secular world, and in the body of Christ.

It is hoped that each of us will be challenged to walk with God in such a way that our loyalty is to him first above all the ways of this world and traditions of men. May we be willing enough to seek God in such a way that we're willing to allow his Holy Spirit to search us and reveal hidden strongholds in our lives.

Our prayer to God ought to be like David's: "Search me, O God, and know my heart; test me and know my anxious thoughts. See if there is any offensive way in me, and lead me in the way everlasting," Psalm 139:23-24.

May we be willing to make the needed changes once God has exposed areas of falsehood we've been embracing. May we be willing to allow the Holy Spirit to pull down these spiritual strongholds and replace them with his word and his ways. The chapters ahead will cover more on this deliverance area.

"The path of the righteous is like the first gleam of dawn, shining ever brighter till the full light of day. But the way of the wicked is like deep darkness; they do not know what makes them stumble,"

Proverbs 4:18-19.

The severity of strongholds: minor, moderate, & extreme

Spiritual strongholds vary in their effects on our lives. This is the case for both types of spiritual strongholds: known and unknown (hidden) strongholds. Each stronghold affects a person in any one of the three ways below:

- Extreme level: Some strongholds are extreme forms of demonic influence that greatly hinder any one or combination of areas in our lives: spiritually, socially, materially, or physically.
- Moderate level: Other strongholds affect us moderately to the extent that we can still effectively fulfill our daily lives.
- Minor level: Other strongholds affect us in a minor way to the extent that their effects have an insignificant impact on our lives.

Below I have listed four examples of strongholds that are extreme forms of demonic influence that can hinder each area of our lives. A life size list can be added to each area. Thus for each person it's worth prayerfully searching for not only the severity of strongholds but also which area(s) of one's life they affect.

1) Strongholds hindering spiritual lives of people: Greed, materialism, worldliness, unforgiveness, bitterness, sexual sins
2) Strongholds hindering social lives of people: Sexual sins, un-forgiveness, bitterness, temper tantrums, materialism, alcohol addiction, discrimination (gender, racial, ethnic, "looks," etc.)
3) Strongholds hindering material lives of people: Greed, selfishness, compulsive gambling
4) Strongholds hindering physical lives of people: Alcohol addiction, unhealthy eating habits, addiction to unhealthy foods.

Dealing with the spiritual strongholds ought to be next once the root causes are found. This book has principles for dealing with both spiritual strongholds and healing the wounded spirit. The two are intertwined and are dealt with in the same way.

Chapter 3:

The Nature of a Wounded, Crushed, or Broken Spirit

What is a wounded spirit?

What is a wounded spirit? It's also known as a broken spirit or crushed spirit. The bible says, "A man's spirit sustains him in sickness, but a crushed spirit who can bear?" Proverbs 18:14. "A cheerful heart is good medicine, but a crushed spirit dries up the bones," Proverbs 17:22.

A wounded spirit is injury to any area of our soul or spirit faculties - mind, emotions and will. It is injury to the unseen areas of our being. The only way others can see the injury is how we behave and conduct ourselves. At least one area inside us may be more affected than the others. The deeper or more severe the wounds the greater the negative effect on an individual's life - spiritually, socially, materially and physically.

As the scripture says a wounded spirit is worse than physical sickness. Physical sickness can be sustained by a healthy spirit but a sick spirit cannot be sustained by anything. Needless to say God is fully able to cure spiritual wounds and heal a sick spirit. He's our spiritual physician or medical doctor. In the chapters ahead we will discuss God's healing work.

The spirit part of us is the engine to our lives. Life is broken when the spirit's health is considerably compromised no matter how attractive, healthy and expensive the body may look. The breakdown of the spirit also eventually brings sickness to the body. The bible says it dries up the bones (*Proverbs 17:22*).

A wounded spirit is not a poor man's bread but affects all economic groups. You've probably heard this: A survey of 65 countries, published by New Scientist (1999-2001, UK), said that people in Nigeria are the happiest people on earth followed by people in Mexico, Venezuela, El Salvador and Puerto Rico respectively. Third world nations took the lead, the USA was 16th.

The survey keeps yielding different results each period and has its human limitations. However it confirms Christ's words: "*A man's life does not consist in the abundance of his possessions,*" Luke *12:15.*

People have rephrased it as: "money cannot buy happiness." The researchers actually described the desire or longing for material wealth as "a happiness suppressant." So those longing for earthly possessions end up less happy and prone to spiritual wounds.

Spiritual attacks, next to social and financial problems cause the worst afflictions to believers and non-believers alike. Some are so severe that the victims end up being ruined spiritually. You have probably heard of references such as nervous wretch, emotional basket case, maniac, psycho, etc. The ruin can be in any area or combination of our inner selves –mind, emotions and will areas.

Scars show healed wounds Vs. those with wounds yet to heal

Spiritual wounds compromise or harm our spiritual health. They potentially can lead to spiritual illness or inner health problems. Two matters determine whether or not these past unpleasant experiences have any negative effect on our present:
1) our reaction to them, and
2) the severity of the experiences.
The degree of their effect varies from person to person and in different areas of our spiritual faculties (mind, emotion and will).

Each of us has some level of scars in our spirits from whatever unpleasant past experiences. Scars imply that the wounds have healed. We can recall the unpleasant experiences and how we had so much inner pain. Occasional recall or remembrance of the experiences only serves as a reminder that we pulled through. God was faithful in enabling us to rise above the experiences instead of leaving us to drown from them.

In the present we've moved on, the past inner hurt and pain is gone. There is no preoccupation with the sad past experiences. They have no power over us, or over our present circumstances. Many times we may also see how God still brought good out of the unpleasant experiences.

It is when the wounds have not healed that it's a problem. It's the opposite of the above scenario. We constantly recall the unpleasant experiences, how unfair they were, and assume we'd be better off today had we not experienced them.

In the present we're still preoccupied with the past, the past inner hurt and pain still surfaces in negative ways. They have power over us and over our present circumstances. Many times we cannot even see how God still brought good out of the unpleasant experiences. The inner wounds are still raw and untreated.

Chapter 4:

There Are Four Doorways Of Access For Spiritual Wounds

The first source of spiritual wounds and strongholds

The sources of spiritual wounds and strongholds are the avenues, or doorways, through which they come through. Satan and his fellow fallen angels use these doorways to gain legal access in their mission or ministry to *"steal and kill and destroy,"* John 10:7. They are also the doorways through which we have a vulnerability of falling due to our own nature, if granted its sinful appetites. These four doorways of access are:
1) deception (covered in this chapter),
2) ignorance,
3) sin, and
4) storms of life when responded to inappropriately

Satan's access through any of these doorways or our falling due to our own sinful nature can result in spiritual wounds as much as it can result in other types of wounds - social, material, and physical. Spiritual wounds are however, the worst because they affect the other areas of life more severely. Spiritual wounds lead to inner ill health or spiritual illness.

It is also worth repeating that any of Satan's access in our lives is through demonic influence. It is not through demonic possession. It is an external type of interference, not an internal one.

The following is detailed info on deception as the most prominent doorway of access for spiritual wounds and other unpleasant matters into our lives. Please remember that spiritual wounds relate to our human spiritual faculties - mind, will, and emotions.

What is deception?

Deception is a deliberate attempt to make something that is false to appear as if it is true. It is a lie made in such a way that the liar deliberately makes it to appear as if it's true. Similar words for deceiving include: lie, snake, mislead, beguile, delude, dupe, defraud, trick, bamboozle, fool, swindle. The person making the lie is called a liar or a deceiver.

It's also important to separate deception from ignorance. Deception concerns wrong thoughts, words, and actions that a person receives or carries out while having some knowledge that they are wrong. Ignorance on the other hand, concerns wrong thoughts, words, and actions that a person receives or carries out while having no knowledge that they are wrong. It is an unknown or unwitting deception, a deception without one's knowledge. This is why knowledge or understanding on key matters in life is so important. Ignorance will be covered in the next chapter.

Concerning deception, the wrong thoughts, words, and actions may be considered wrong from different perspectives. That list includes from a:

1) moral perspective;
2) cultural perspective;
3) a legal perspective;
4) physical/health perspective;
5) religious perspective;
6) or any combination of the above.

It is the religious perspective that's more important for us Christians. Applying the Christian faith in its true sense, with God's Spirit effectively working in our lives, fulfills all fundamental human perspectives.

"The fruit of the Spirit is love, joy, peace, patience, kindness, goodness, faithfulness, gentleness and self-control. Against such things there is no law. Those who belong to Christ Jesus have crucified the sinful nature with its passions and desires," Galatians 5:22-24

How does conscience work in people?

In every scenario leading to deception there's an inner voice opposing the deceptive thoughts. The inner voice says why it is not worth carrying out the thoughts and actions. This inner voice is called the conscience.

A conscience is easier to illustrate than to define. It is our personal judge that gives us the sense of what's right and what's wrong. It is a moral compass in us that works more from our emotions, rather than the mental side. The conscience uses the mind in guiding and revealing the moral basis. However it uses our emotions in creating an inner atmosphere that facilitates an avoidance of poor thought, ill speech or wrong doing.

When we think, say, or do anything that's wrong our conscience rings a prolonged emotional bell in us that we've gone the wrong way. The emotional bell it rings is called guilt. Guilt makes us feel sad, unpleasant or shamed and it encourages us to make up for or correct the wrong. A person with a healthy conscience will experience some level of guilt for these actions. This is why someone is said to have a "guilty conscience" when he/she has said or done something wrong.

Genuine guilt is healthy to a certain level. Guilt is the emotional voice response from our conscience that enables us to continue, or get back to, behavior consistent with our beliefs and values. When we think or attempt to say or to do something contrary to our conscience a sense of guilt wells up within us condemning us and insisting we do or say the right thing.

Most people have a working conscience. This is the case even for non-Christians. It's just that unbelievers do not have the extra backing of the Holy Spirit to convict their conscience if they attempt to stray or end up straying from what's right.

The bible says about unbelievers (Gentiles), "Indeed, when Gentiles, who do not have the law, do by nature things required by the law, they are a law for themselves, even though they do not have the law, since they show that the requirements of the law are written on their hearts, their consciences also bearing witness, and their thoughts now accusing, now even defending them," Romans 2:14-15.

Thus everybody has a conscience. The only question is, what percentage of their conscience is operating? For some it's 10%, others 40%, still others 95%. Only God can accurately measure the weight of each person's conscience on each matter in life.

Some people have a higher sense of consciousness or awareness in matters dealing with the poor, others with children, physical health, the environment, animals, morality in general, civil rights, or even politics; the list goes on. For us Christians our sense of consciousness ought to be highest on spiritual issues, focusing on the spiritual poverty for those who have not yet received salvation through Christ. Then followed by other needs of our fellow humanity – physical health needs, material needs, psychosocial needs, etc. The rest may take third place.

Being a Christian does not automatically translate into being pure, godly and holy. It does, however, open an opportunity that unbelievers do not have. This opportunity is being under the influence of the Holy Spirit. The Holy Spirit gives a bigger boost to our conscience by making us receive the heart of God once we become born again.

"I will give you a new heart and put a new spirit in you; I will remove from you your heart of stone and give you a heart of flesh. And I will put my Spirit in you and move you to follow my decrees and be careful to keep my laws," Ezekiel 36:26-27.

The dilemma lies in that lack of an automatic transition into being pure, godly and holy. That transition requires our input and willingness to cooperate with the Holy Spirit in embracing this new nature. God through the Holy Spirit does not remote control us without our consent. He respects our free will (as Almighty as he is) and has thus chosen to work alongside our willingness.

What about a seared or burnt conscience?

Although most people have at least a working conscience some do not have a healthy conscience. The bible speaks of people "whose consciences have been seared as with a hot iron," 1 Timothy 4: 2.

A person with a seared, or burnt, conscience is one that does not feel guilty for doing wrong. He cares little about other people's interests and primarily only thinks about his self-centered interests.

The conscience becomes seared when inner convictions of right and wrong are rejected on a constant basis so that an individual blunts the conscience. It becomes dull, deadened, compromised, or ineffectual. The conscience grows weaker and more silent in the individual.

With a dull conscience a person ends up experiencing little to no guilt for any wrong thoughts, words or actions. Thus he's not able to have what is commonly called a "guilty conscience," for committing a wrong. A person who's able to experience little or no guilt over fulfilling a wrong desire becomes an easy vessel for deception. The level a person has compromised his/her conscience to become seared will determine the extent a person will give in to deception. The higher the compromise the more he/she will be willing to embrace wrong matters.

Think about it, a petty thief who snatches wallets and handbags has a less weak conscience than a criminal who's ready to kill for gain, or a person in the business world who is willing to harm the moral, physical or material lives of masses. A pimp whose business is supplying prostitutes to willing clients has compromised his conscience more than the prostitutes he manages.

The same can be said of some people with higher influence who compromise their consciences: top politicians, business people, media executives, educational heads, entertainment executives, and others with extensive influence on masses. Being given much responsibility and a higher accountability is expected from them. Some, but not all, compromise their accountability for self-gain.

"When someone has been given much, much will be required in return; and when someone has been entrusted with much, even more will be required," Luke 12:48.

Can a Christian have a seared or burnt conscience?

A Christian cannot have a seared conscience unless he/she has willfully fallen out of the faith. A person can depart from the Christian faith. This takes a lot of serious wrong choices knowingly and after ignoring repeated convictions from the Holy Spirit. How else can we explain those who were once in the faith and now want nothing to do with Christianity?

"The Spirit clearly says that in later times some will abandon the faith and follow deceiving spirits and things taught by demons," 1 Timothy 4:1.

Needless to say that there is still hope of return for such individuals, and that a person has left the Christian faith does not automatically imply he/she now has a seared conscience.

Three sources of deception

As stated earlier in this chapter, deception is the most prominent doorway for spiritual wounds. It is defined as wrong thoughts, words, and actions that a person receives or carries out while having some knowledge that doing so is in fact wrong. There are three sources of deception:

1) Deception through deceiving spirits (fallen angels)
2) Deception through ourselves (self-deception)
3) Deception through other people:
   a. In the World
   b. In the Church

1) Deception through deceiving spirits (fallen angels, demons)

In the spirit realm fallen angels are the source of deception. The greatest deceiver of all time is Satan. He and his fellow fallen angels (demons) are called deceiving spirits. *"The Spirit clearly says that in later times some will abandon the faith and follow deceiving spirits and things taught by demons," 1 Timothy 4:1.*

The Holy Spirit is the *"Spirit of truth"* (*John 16:13*) while demons are deceiving spirits. The two spiritual camps are complete opposites in their work. Satan and his fellow fallen angels are the ultimate deceivers in all the depravity in this world. The Holy Spirit on the other hand is the ultimate conveyer of truth convicting each person through his/her conscience on what's right and what's wrong.

Why is there the Holy Spirit single handedly doing his work of conveying the truth verses so many fallen angels doing their work of endeavoring to deceive people? It's because the Holy Spirit is omnipresent. Omnipresence is only the ability of God in his Trinitarian nature (the Father, Son and Holy Spirit). All angels, that is, God's angels and fallen angels (including Satan) are created spirits with geographical limitation. Each angel (good or evil) can only be in one place at one time, not several places at the same time.

Thus evil spirits being able to only be in one place at a time assign themselves to each person in a particular area. Each evil spirit strives to succeed in deceiving an individual it has targeted in a particular matter. If it succeeds the individual is said to be deceived. The street terms are duped, bamboozled and fooled.

Being in this fallen world all of us have fallen to some form or other of deception at some point in our lives. Deceiving spirits do have their areas of success in each of us. Fortunately we have the Holy Spirit. This is such a blessing. The Holy Spirit is God inside each of us. He is the Spirit that equips us with the truth against all the lies that deceiving spirits constantly throw at us.

Deceiving spirits, including Satan, do not operate the same way they did in the Garden of Eden. We do not see snakes or other animals talking to us with evil intent. Satan and his evil team endeavor to work against us in the unseen spirit realm. However we're also to be mindful that there are more forces from God's kingdom in the spirit realm than Satan's forces. God's angels outnumber fallen angels by a 3 to 1 ratio. When Satan rebelled he somehow persuaded one-third of the other angels to join him (*Revelation 12:3-4*). Fallen angels are no match against God's angels. That is why the bible says, *"Those who are with us are more than those who are with them...Then the Lord opened the servant's eyes, and he looked and saw the hills full of horses and chariots of fire all round Elisha,"* 2 Kings 6:16-17.

Thus we're not to be afraid that evil spirits or fallen angels are plotting against us. We have more spiritual forces on our side working to stop their evil schemes. When fallen angels succeed in deceiving a person the result is that the person will follow their proposals instead of God's proposal. In other ways, the person will sin against God. This is what Adam and Eve did when they bought Satan's lies and abandoned God's truth. As Christians we have extra strength at work in us to overcome such attempts. May our abiding in Christ be healthy enough to overcome the lies from deceiving spirits.

2. Deception through ourselves (self-deception)

Having the fallen nature makes us naturally imperfect. Some of the deception that people experience is self-made. It is true that Satan and his fellow deceiving spirits do labor to take advantage of our fallen nature. However, there are instances where it is purely out of our own exercise of the freedom of choice that results in willful wrong choices. In such instances demons play no role in influencing us.

Remember that evil spirits, including Satan, cannot read our minds. Remember all angels, whether fallen angels or God's angels, are incapable of reading our minds. They are created beings that God limited in their abilities. Fallen angels are able to whisper corrupt ideas to our minds but they do not know what we're thinking in our minds. The only way they can later tell is through the way we respond to the ideas they try to plant.

If fallen angels could read our minds they would not have influenced the crucifixion of Jesus. Jesus knew his mission yet fallen angels, including Satan, had no idea of what was ahead. Fallen angels remained ignorant even when Jesus preached about his mission many times. His crucifixion marked their ultimate downfall. Had they known exactly what Jesus knew, they would not have influenced Jesus' opponents to crucify him.

Satan, and other fallen angels, being unable to read our minds cannot control what and how we think. We're in charge of the thinking process, what preoccupies us and how we respond to our thoughts. That is why everyone, including unbelievers, will be judged on how they acted upon the thoughts in their minds. God gave us full custody over our own minds and will judge us on how we allowed our minds to do the things we did, good or bad. Satan will not be part of the excuse. Our biggest enemy is therefore within us. It is our own fallen nature.

Some of the matters we think on and how we think on them are due to the fallen nature that we inherited from Adam and Eve. God cursed Adam and consequently all humanity after he sinned in the Garden of Eden. The whole world, including us God's children is under the curse of the Original Sin. Such a curse is better called the fallen nature, the corrupted nature, the flesh, etc. The fallen nature is what makes us imperfect physically in our health and looks, and spiritually in our minds, understanding and behavior. In our minds this fallen nature can be seen through the following thoughts and actions:

1) self-centeredness,
2) greed,
3) pride,
4) territorialism,
5) materialism,
6) lustfulness,
7) gluttony,
8) jealousy,
9) anger,
10) vengeance,
11) unforgiveness,
12) laziness,
13) workaholics.

"When tempted, no one should say, "God is tempting me." For God cannot be tempted by evil, nor does he tempt anyone; but each one is tempted when, by his own evil desire, he is dragged away and enticed. Then, after desire has conceived, it gives birth to sin; and sin, when it is full-grown, gives birth to death," James 1:13-15.

Notice in the passage that it says a person is tempted by his own evil desire. It does not say tempted by Satan. There is a realm of temptation and wrong thinking that can go on in our minds without any input from evil spirits. The wrong or bad thoughts that go on in our minds without any input from evil spirits are what constitute our own evil desires. They are products of our own fallen nature.

"Those who live according to the sinful nature have their minds set on what that nature desires; but those who live in accordance with the Spirit have their minds set on what the Spirit desires. The mind of sinful man is death, but the mind controlled by the Spirit is life and peace; the sinful mind is hostile to God. It does not submit to God's law, nor can it do so. Those controlled by the sinful nature cannot please God," Romans 8:5-8.

Notice the distinction between the "sinful mind" and the new nature. They are opposites. The "sinful mind" is "set on what that nature desires" while the new nature is a "mind controlled by the Spirit." One is self-controlled by the inborn fallen nature while the other mind is powered by the Holy Spirit.

Therefore, we should all need the Holy Spirit to help us to restrain the fallen nature from having its wishes. Salvation is the first step. Obedience to God's word and the inner promptings of the Holy Spirit is the ultimate step.

Philosophy, psychology and other noble human fields cannot work to restrain the fallen nature from having its wishes. Neither can socialism, communism, and worse, capitalism, work to tame the flesh. Other religions preach goodness, cooperation, love and charity, yet they have no power over the flesh. As well intentioned as they may be only the Holy Spirit who gives us the new nature, the new mind of Christ, is able to tame the flesh.

Having settled that our own fallen nature does exist and shown how it works we should now move on to defining self-deception. A good definition of self-deception is given by Wikipedia, an online encyclopedia. It says, "Self-deception is a process of denying or rationalizing away the relevance, significance, or importance of opposing evidence and logical argument," (Wikimedia Foundation, Inc., Wikipedia, "Self-deception"). From a Christian perspective we can say self-deception is a process of denying or rationalizing away the relevance, significance, or importance of promptings from the inner conscience in order to satisfy the desires of the fallen nature.

The definition is this straightforward. Self-deception is basically self propaganda. Propaganda is deceptive or distorted information that is tactfully spread or broadcasted to people in order to promote a false idea, cause, policy, or doctrine. In relation to self propaganda or self-deception a person acts to convince himself that fulfilling a false or wrong matter is good or worthwhile.

Here are a few quotations that illustrate the unredeemed and unrestrained fallen nature:

1) "Man's mind is so formed that it is far more susceptible to falsehood than to truth," by Desiderius Erasmus ((1466-1536) Dutch theologian).
2) "No man was ever so much deceived by another as by himself," by Brook Fulke Greville (1554 - 1628)
3) "A fraudulent intent, however carefully concealed at the outset, will generally, in the end, betray itself," by Titus Livius (Livy).

This is why humanity so desperately needs the heart of God. People remain vulnerable to sinful ways without the heart of God. God's spiritual heart comes through salvation and through the inner filling (anointing) of the Holy Spirit.

"I will give you a new heart and put a new spirit in you; I will remove from you your heart of stone and give you a heart of flesh. And I will put my Spirit in you and move you to follow my decrees and be careful to keep my laws," Ezekiel 36:26-27.

People without a new heart remain vulnerable to the influence of the human fallen nature and to evil spirits (fallen angels). Some would collapse from shock if I were to chronicle the wickedness in many of the world's highest levels of politics, business, the media, and other influential areas. But the right time for much hidden matters will be at the end of time when all things will be revealed to us. Everything will be revealed, including our own lives and the deep secrets of those in high places.

3a) Deception through other people in the World

Not only do we have to confront deception from ourselves through the fallen nature and deception from deceiving spirits, we also have to confront deception from our fellow humanity.

Deception from other people can be influenced by their own fallen nature or they could be influenced by deceiving spirits. It is largely not our business trying to find what's influencing them to attempt to deceive others. For the most part we'd only be guessing on whether the deception was influenced by the person's own fallen nature or by deceiving spirits. It also matters less on knowing what influenced a person to deceive than knowing the effect, or impact, of the deception on other people. Knowing the effect of any deception on other people is important because it helps us to work on assembling the truth against the deception.

Telling people that they're being deceived by their fallen nature or by deceiving spirits may only work to irritate them. They'll be annoyed with your self-righteous overtures and why you're trying to be their judge. The story changes when you share the truth on matters that they are being deceived on.

In most cases, people who intentionally seek to deceive others take advantage of their ignorance. When the truth is shared on what others are ignorant from it safeguards them from being deceived. Once they know the truth in an area of potential deception the only way they can fall for the lies is by willfully embracing them. Those who end up falling in this category basically end up being partners with the deceivers.

The bible says, "Evil men and impostors will go from bad to worse, deceiving and being deceived," 2 Timothy 3:13. Evil people are those with wrong motives in life, always willing to gain even through taking advantage of others. Impostors are people who pretend to be something that they really are not.

The easiest area to give examples of impostors is in politics. They're willing to express what their target segment of voters want. Sometimes they are even willing to put some action to what they claim to believe in. In actual fact what they believe in is acquisition of power above being of service to the electorate. Their thirst for wielding power and influence is later found out once elected into office. Their fruits or behavior reveals them. They shift to the usual politics: representing the interests of the wealthy and powerful groups with little to no constructive regard for the masses.

How many politicians have you come across that after being elected have not fallen into the status quo? They find themselves getting into politics as usual. Even some that may have breakthrough ideas and desires they find out that the system is bigger than them. They find themselves bowing to the wishes of those who rule by secrecy and actually have power and influence in the system. Many find themselves representing Mystery Babylon.

This scenario is not only a feature of developing nations. In developed nations the political system has graduated to using the most sophisticated methods of maintaining the status quo. If one wants to master the crafts of deception they'd be in a good position learning the principles from some developed nations. I won't pick any names but instead leave you to do your own research on this one.

The methods used are so sophisticated that it takes an investigative mind to uncover them. Notice I didn't say it takes a university or college mind to uncover them. Andy Rooney says, *"You meet a lot of dumb people who went to college,"* (Andy Rooney, "Common Nonsense: Addressed to the Reading Public," p.137). I too have a number of university degrees so no Christian in the academia ought to take any offense for this statement.

The main status quo that even well intentioned and noble politicians find themselves bowing to is that of guarding the interests of the rich and powerful. The rich and powerful in this context are not the Hollywood actors, musicians, or other wealthy and famous people in the entertainment world. These are just blinders to divert people's attention from those who really have worldly wealth, power and influence. They're not public figures for the most part. They rule in secrecy, a real biblical testament of the end-times.

The list of tools used to endeavor to deceive masses include some of the most obvious and even more of the least obvious. Someone around 2003 described them as "weapons of mass deception." All along many have called them propaganda machines. Although the public deception tools can be listed, the methods of using them are not clear-cut. They are for the most part sophisticated and highly secretive.

The most obvious propaganda machine is the media. In most countries, developed and developing nations, the media is primarily owned by a few players. In developing nations the primary or dominant owners are the government, owning the greatest share of the media pie. In most developed nations the primary owners are a handful of corporations (large private companies). These few media corporations have unholy alliances with other giant private corporations, such as in banking, technology, pharmaceutical industry, food industry, oil industry, and many more.

Thus in both scenarios, of developed and developing nations, media ownership is controlled by a few key players. Worldwide, this trend has been growing and not diminishing, in the last 50 years. It is another biblical testament of the end-times.

Media ownership is very important real estate. The real estate that the media controls is the minds of people. Gone are the days of using physical force to influence and control people. The "civilized" way now is to use information that gets to them. This smarter way dawned after those that have motives of power, control and influence began to learn from the noble fields of psychology, sociology and other related fields of study. They learned the principles from these fields and began to use them for deceitful reasons. They keep improving their skills as time, increasing technological advancements, and experience helps them.

Some of the least obvious tools that are part of the propaganda machine are books, the educational system, the internet, and the principles of divide and rule. The internet however, is also working against them. A great deal of suppressed information is abundantly available online.

For example, on the educational system, countries have entire government ministries of education, culture and other branches. For the most part the ministries have a lot of positive contributions. On the negative side some of what they decide as the standard of instruction ends up being distorted to suite whatever goals they have. Anything that one distorts ends up losing its truthful validity, objectivity, and true meaning.

Here is an example from countries I can easily relate with. When Zambia and Zimbabwe got their independence they embarked on indigenization programs to transform the countries from colonial rule to independent countries. Part of the indigenization programs included transforming the educational system. Previously what was taught as history was distorted and biased to suit the biases of the colonial governments. This was quickly changed, now it is biased to suit the biases of the independent nations. The change may have been valid to remove the previous biases. The problem, however, concerns the creation of another bias. Zambia and Zimbabwe are merely examples to show that deception is all around us. No country can claim any innocence. Not even the Vatican, the world's smallest independent nation and headquarters of the Roman Catholic Church.

Napoleon Bonaparte, a 19th century legendary French ruler said, "What is history but a fable agreed upon?" (1769-1821). He said this in the 19th century. How much more does this apply in our 21st century where information about the past and the present is major real estate for power and influence?

"The falsification of history has done more to impede human development than any one thing known to mankind," by Rousseau 1712-1778.

"After you've heard two eyewitness accounts of an auto accident, you begin to worry about history," by an unknown author.

As Christians we're expected to rise above human biases that only serve to continue dividing us, whether by race, nationality or gender. More importantly we're expected to rise above the deception that is sweeping through the media, some parts of news, some entertainment, etc. Just one look at the entertainment world shows Christianity is far from the life they are promoting. The entertainment world has largely grown to be a tool to serve three main purposes. Christianity is not one of them:

1) To promote consumerism and materialism to make people to keep spending on bling bling (material goods) produced by the big business world (corporations),

2) To influence people into adopting certain beliefs and behaviors (such as accepting sex outside marriage, unfaithfulness, homosexuality, magnifying and playing on our insignificant human differences for divide and rule purposes),

3) To serve as a tool of distraction, diversion, or interference from focusing on matters that are really important to the masses: empowerment, equal opportunity, dealing with poverty, health-care, crime, discrimination (gender, age, race, ethnicity and economic).

Here are some quotations that relate to deception and our need to be vigilant:

- *"A simple man believes anything, but a prudent man gives thought to his steps," Proverbs 14:15.*
- "Politicians are masters of the art of deception," by Martin L. Gross.
- "In order to become the master, the politician poses as the servant," by Charles de Gaulle (1890-1970) French politician.
- "Nothing is as admirable in politics as a short memory (of the masses)," by John K. Galbraith (1908-2006) Canadian born economist.

- "Catch-22 says they have a right to do anything we can't stop them from doing," by Joseph Heller (1923-1999) author, USA.
- "Never forget that everything Hitler did in Germany was legal," (i.e. anything considered legal doesn't necessarily make it right) by Martin Luther King Jr., Church minister and civil rights leader, USA
- "It's useless to hold a person to anything he says while he's (madly) in love, drunk or running for office," by Shirley McLain (1934-) actress, USA.
- "There are two kinds of statistics, the kind you look up, and the kind you make up," by Rex Stout (1886-1975) writer, USA.
- "What is the difference between unethical and ethical advertising? Unethical advertising uses falsehoods to deceive the public; ethical advertising uses truth to deceive the public," by Vilhjalmur Stefansson.
- "Racism keeps people who are being managed from finding out the truth through contact with each other," by Shirley Chisholm (b. 1924), African American politician, USA.

I have used politics and the big business world as examples to illustrate what deception from other people is. It is not intended to cause fear in you. It has been shared to make you aware of behind-the-scenes matters going on this world. If taken for granted these matters have the potential to wreck havoc on our Christian lives. Expect the matters to happen in this fallen world for three major reasons:

1) They were prophesied to come to pass,
2) They are natural or instinctive acts of the fallen nature that people without the new nature given by the Holy Spirit are vulnerable to, and,
3) Satan and his fallen angels endeavor to exploit or to take advantage of the fallen nature in people.

Notice I said expect them to happen in this fallen world, not accept them to happen in this fallen world. As you know expect and accept are two different words meaning two entirely different things.

As Christians we're not to accept the matters to happen in this fallen world. This is in spite of expecting them to happen due to the three reasons outlined above. We're to refuse them from influencing us and from influencing others. It's not enough to feel safe that we've been rescued from them – at least spiritually. We've a mandate to rescue others from matters that work to destroy them in the long-run. The most important matters are those that concern their spiritual lives. Yes there are matters bringing people down in their material lives and physical health as well. However it is their spiritual lives that ought to be our biggest concern. Through evangelism of the gospel we make known God's truths about their spiritual lives and their eternal destiny.

This is why many of us in the body of Christ cannot be politicians. Politics has to do with temporal things of "bread and butter." As noble as it sounds to have a godly and born again person in top political office it's not God's major priority. Otherwise God could have brought down many of the big business-serving and greedy politicians in this world. He would have easily exalted many of the godly and born again people willing to serve in the political field.

3b) Deception through other people in the Church

People from the secular world are by no means the only potential culprits of being sources of deception. Other people right close to each of us can potentially attempt to deceive us if their intentions are not well aligned to the scriptures.

Yes, we too can deceive others if our desires and intentions are not well aligned. But let's focus on deception in the church or the body of Christ from leadership positions.

In the body of Christ, for the most part, people who deceive others do it out of one or any combination of the following reasons:

1) They are themselves deceived (whether through deceiving spirits, self-deception, or deceived through other people in the church), or

2) Out of a desire to embrace the ways of this fallen world compromise or twist the scriptures to suite their aims. They also compromise the Christian fundamental tenets and focus primarily on teachings that are peripheral or secondary in the Christian faith.

The most prominent of such deceptive teachings in our times include glorification of earthly riches, worldly pleasures, power, and status. In such circles people are so preoccupied with their material success, comforts, and welfare that the major Christian concerns become secondary. In many cases the major Christian concerns are seen as tools to serve their own long-term welfare.

For example, a person may perceive being generous and giving offering primarily as a means to end up receiving more in return. The primary motive that God expects of us, that of an inner desire to make a difference in the lives of others becomes secondary. This is materialism packaged with a Christian face by using selective bible verses that are itchy to our ears.

"For the time will come when men will not put up with sound doctrine. Instead, to suit their own desires, they will gather around them a great number of teachers to say what their itching ears want to hear. They will turn their ears away from the truth and turn aside to myths," 2 Timothy 4:3-4).

"I urge you, brothers, to watch out for those who cause divisions and put obstacles in your way that are contrary to the teaching you have learned. Keep away from them. For such people are not serving our Lord Christ, but their own appetites. By smooth talk and flattery they deceive the minds of naive people," Rom. 16:17-18.

For some it's out of compromise to make the message of the gospel more pleasing to certain groups. Instead of sticking with God's standard some choose to embrace the people's standards. It could be out of financial reasons to keep the offering flowing or out of wanting to please people without offending anyone.

Some who fail to live up to Christian standards of righteousness, holiness, love, charity and other Christian disciplines end up projecting their compromised standards to other people. Thus out of personal failures of living up to the righteousness requirements in God's word some adopt the lukewarm gospel. Their teachings are variously labeled as the liberal gospel, lukewarm gospel, all grace gospels, and once saved always saved gospel. This all grace gospel with little personal input or responsibility is a major form of deception that is a thorn in the body of Christ.

Compromising of ideals of the Christian faith works to even eliminate the chances of some people to make it to heaven. "For I tell you that unless your righteousness surpasses that of the Pharisees and the teachers of the law, you will certainly not enter the kingdom of heaven," Matthew 5:20. Modern Pharisees are leading masses to follow their own carved out Christianity. Sadly they block the chances of entering into God's kingdom not just for themselves but also for those they minister to.

Apostle Paul, God's prominent early church vessel said he strived to enter into God's kingdom so that he would not be disqualified. In other words, he wanted to make it as much as he wanted others to make it. If ever he failed to make it he would not lower the Christian ideals to mirror his own personal failures. We know that he made it.

Like Paul and other servants of God, it's also my prayer that I make it. If ever (God forbid) my own commitment to the Christian ideals is compromised I would not resort to lowering the standards to those God reaches through me. I'd rather be the only one to fail to make it than take many others with me to the spiritual failures' world.

Neither will I be enticed to preach teachings that exalt material success above spiritual success. I would quietly pursue earthly riches without showing or proclaiming it to vulnerable believers that driving the latest Mercedes or having a private jet is fulfilling the ultimate dream in this life. It is fulfilling the ultimate lie in this life. By God's grace and the power of choice he has given me I'll not fall for such. I will thus make it into heaven as much as those God uses me to minister his pure truths to.

"Therefore I run thus: not with uncertainty. Thus I fight: not as one who beats the air. But I discipline my body and bring it into subjection, lest, when I have preached to others, I myself should become disqualified," 1 Corinthians 9:26-27.

Through occult infiltration into Christianity, some deceptive and false teachings end up in the body of Christ. There are some occult groups with an agenda to destroy Christianity. The most prominent among these groups are Freemasons. Ralph Epperson, in his book, "Masonry: Conspiracy Against Christianity-- Evidence That the Masonic Lodge Has a Secret Agenda", covers how Freemasons are working against Christianity.

The position where they're most able to broadcast and market their false teachings are pastoral or church leadership positions.

So their focus is to work from the top influential positions in order to choke Christianity's spiritual power. From the top influential positions they're also able to influence not only church members but other church leaders and church bodies. Many of them secretly use financial resources specifically allocated for infiltrating Christianity from their Freemasonry group.

This is how some of them are able to rise to high prominence in the body of Christ. Such prominence gives them easy legitimacy and can claim that they're genuine Christians. It also makes their teachings easily adoptable by genuine Christian leaders who admire the secret infiltrator.

Since the infiltrator seems like a genuine Christian some Christian leaders end up adopting his teachings without question and without any sound biblical scrutiny. In the long run the body of Christ ends up being littered with false teachings that the secret infiltrator introduced. My other book on breaking occult curses has more detailed info on how this works and what role we can play in doing our part to safeguard ourselves and the body of Christ.

In almost all cases where people are being taught matters that are deceptive there is an insulated mindset. I've been there too, so it's a very familiar scenario. The people are so closed in their own box of perspectives and understanding that they shield themselves from any other different Christian perspective.

Their minds are made up. They are not even going to go through a doctrinal analysis. Thus their minds unconsciously work in defense mode to their understanding with little or no openness to biblical analysis. This scenario has historically happened in all denominational circles in the body of Christ. No church body has been immune.

When a church body or a Christian as an individual adopts an insulated mindset to erroneous teachings there is what can be called self-propaganda. Below is a good definition of self propaganda that beautifully sums up what I'm talking about:

"Self propaganda is a form of propaganda and indoctrination performed by an individual or a group on oneself. Essentially, it is the act of telling yourself. or a group telling themselves, something that they consider to be true, or to convince themselves, with the unfortunate repercussion of their having no doubts.

"Because of what they do to themselves, they will go over every aspect of their side of the "argument" to prove to themselves that they are right, and will refuse to look at any alternatives. Self propaganda is a form of self-deception and indoctrination. It functions at individual and social levels: political, economic, and religious. It hides behind partial truths and ignores questions of critical thought," (Wikimedia Foundation, Inc., Wikipedia, "Self propaganda".

Most teachings that are "itching" to the ears do not go through critical biblical analysis. They appeal to the emotions and those that embrace them move on to find scriptures to justify their understanding. The scriptures they use are either taken out of context or are made to seem as if they are paramount tenets of our Christian faith.

Taking scriptures out of context is not critical biblical analysis. It is critical biblical carelessness. Scripture can be used to justify almost any matter but it does not necessarily imply it is being applied or interpreted correctly. Didn't Satan also use the bible in trying to tempt and deceive Jesus? Wasn't the bible used for centuries to justify subjugation of women, certain ethnic groups and non-Christians?

The ministers who preach this gospel, knowingly projecting their compromised standards to other people, end up falling in the category of false prophets or modern day Pharisees.

Chapter 5:

The Other 3 Sources of Spiritual Wounds & Strongholds

Ignorance, Sin, and Storms of Life

This chapter covers on other three doorways of access or sources for spiritual wounds, strongholds, and other unpleasant matters into our lives. Sources of spiritual wounds and strongholds are avenues or doorways through which they come through. They are doorways Satan and his fellow fallen angels use to gain legal access in their mission or ministry to *"steal and kill and destroy,"* *John 10:7*. They are also doorways through which we've a vulnerability of falling due to our own fallen nature, if granted its sinful appetites. These remaining three doorways of access are through:
1) ignorance,
2) sin, and
3) storms of life, when responded to in an improper way

Satan's permitted access through any of these doorways or our falling due to our own sinful nature. This fall can result in spiritual wounds as much as it can result in other types of wounds - social, material, and physical. Spiritual wounds are however, the worst because they affect the other areas of life more severely. Spiritual wounds lead to inner ill health or spiritual illness. It's also worth repeating that any of Satan's access in our lives is through demonic influence. It is not through demonic possession. It is an external type of interference, not an internal one.

1) Ignorance

It is important to separate deception from ignorance. Deception concerns wrong thoughts, words, and actions that a person receives or carries out while having some knowledge that the thoughts, words, or actions are wrong. Unlike deception, ignorance concerns wrong thoughts, words, and actions that a person receives or carries out while having no knowledge that they are wrong. It is unknown deception or deception without one's knowledge.

This is why knowledge or understanding on key matters in life is so important. Ignorance or lack of knowledge makes one vulnerable to fall victim to all the sources of deception: Satan and his fellow deceiving spirits, self-deception through one's own flesh and deception from people.

Ignorance is therefore an open door for deception. Lack of knowledge can be an open door to adopting all kinds of dangerous beliefs, false doctrines and teachings with the assumption that they are biblical. This results in all kinds of problems related to the false matters one is embracing. The harm one could experience can be in any area(s) of his/her life: spiritual, social, physical health, or material health.

"My people are destroyed from lack of knowledge," Hosea 4:6.

Ignorance is a form of mental slavery that renders a person to be vulnerable to exploitation in the area of ignorance. This is why the scripture says lack of knowledge leads to destruction in any area of one's life: spiritual, social, physical health, or material health.

God's people, not those whose father is the devil (*John 8:44*) are destroyed from lack of knowledge. God's people are destroyed not because Satan is strong and furious. It is because they lack knowledge in areas Satan, his fellow fallen angels, and malicious people are able to gain access. Once knowledge in the area of concern is acquired the exploitations a Christian struggled with come to an end. The needed knowledge in the area of concern brings freedom.

"You will know the truth, and the truth will set you free," John 8:32.

2) Sin

Whether committed knowingly or out of ignorance sin has the same consequences. Sin, in a most basic definition, is either deception yielded to or ignorance in application. This is why deception had to be addressed at length. Once a person knows the nature of deception the battle is half-won. The other half of the battle is in having the inner strength to triumph over the deception.

The solution for sins done out of ignorance is acquiring the necessary truth in the area one is unknowingly falling victim to. Knowing the truth is a major step to receiving freedom. "You will know the truth, and the truth will set you free," John 8:32. Once a person knows the truth in an area of concern the only way he/she can fall is by turning away from the truth. Once this happens we say the person has fallen to deception. The trap of deception becomes the main cause for the sin, not ignorance at this stage.

Sins that can bring a wounded spirit include involvement in occult practices, sexual sins, unforgiveness of past hurts, and severe conflicts between a parent and a child.

3) Storms of Life (when responded to in an improper way)

Storms of life are unpleasant experiences that befall us out of no fault of our own. These include experiences of:

1) betrayal by a loved one; trusted person, or leader;
2) death of a loved one;
3) experiences of severe physical or emotional abuse;
4) living under a heavily controlled disciplinary environment

that brings fear;

5) living under constant negative and critical words;
6) living under rejection;
7) false accusations;
8) terrible divorce experience, as the victim;
9) traumatic experience(s), (e.g. surviving the September 11 terror experience (in Kenya, Tanzania, and USA);
10) traumatic accident, (e.g. casualty of war);
11) having a physical or social disability;
12) having a certain physical appearance society "persecutes;"
13) severe racial, gender and ethnic discrimination or abuse;
14) falling victim to false teachings;
15) genuine trials of faith.

Depending on how we handle them, storms of life can be stepping stones to our promotion, like with Joseph, or they can be our downfall. They can be assets the Holy Spirit can use to our good or they can be assets Satan can use to block us from moving forward.

History has amazing examples of people who ended up in a palace of life instead of a prison of life through the storms they went through. The storms failed to enslave them. God can do awesome work with matters that ordinarily disadvantage us if we trust him to be more powerful than our limitations.

Chapter 6:

Effects of a Wounded Spirit (Broken or Crushed Spirit)

The Original Wounds & their Byproducts (Secondary Wounds)

Spiritual wounds have their original or initial effects and also have their byproducts. Their byproducts are secondary wounds or effects from the original experience(s).

An individual may have effectively healed from being tormented by the bad past yet may behave in some way that could be linked to the experience. The original experience is also no longer a preoccupation nor a source of pain. The individual may even have totally forgiven the wrong doers, if he had been holding bitter feelings.

You have probably heard of Dorothy Law Nolte's famous poem: Children Learn What They Live. It talks about the outcomes that result from parenting styles, good and bad styles. Here's the poem:

If a child lives with criticism, he learns to condemn...
If a child lives with hostility, he learns to fight...
If a child lives with fear, he learns to be apprehensive...
If a child lives with pity, he learns to feel sorry for himself...
If a child lives with ridicule, he learns to be shy...
If a child lives with jealousy, he learns to feel guilt...
BUT
If a child lives with tolerance, he learns to be patient...
If a child lives with encouragement, he learns to be confident...
If a child lives with, he learns to be appreciative...
If a child lives with acceptance, he learns to love...

If a child lives with honesty, he learns what truth is...
If a child lives with fairness, he learns justice...
If a child lives with security, he learns to have faith in himself and those about him...
If a child lives with friendliness, he learns the world is a nice place in which to live...

By the way we're all children no matter how old we get. We just learn to better deal with the negative matters in life as we grow. Some learn better than others. As believers we've the most solid foundation in life: God's word. We're expected to ignore the lies from demonic influence trying to exalt the bad past over God's word.

The above poem is a good illustration in showing spiritual wounds and their byproducts. In the poem the spiritual wounds are the negative factors the child experiences: criticism, hostility, fear, pity, ridicule, and jealousy. We can add much more to the list. Each factor can also result in more than one outcome. Thus a spiritual wound inflicted on a person may result in one or more negative outcomes. It is a seed sown, albeit a bad seed, that produces its bigger harvest, albeit a sour harvest.

For example, a child that's under constant criticism may grow up being judgmental, hostile, and fearful. Most of these outcomes fall in the category of byproducts to spiritual wounds. They're not the original spiritual wounds themselves but are the consequence or effects of the original wounds.

A person may be totally be free from the torment of the past, holding no grudges against anyone that may have caused some bad past experiences. He has been healed from the pain of the original wounds. However he may still need healing from the consequences or effects of the wounds. Healing from byproducts of spiritual wounds is exactly the same way as in healing from the original spiritual wounds. The effects are actually spiritual wounds only in a secondary or byproduct manner. A few factors are original spiritual wounds themselves. For instance, frequent recurring memories of a past hurt are an aspect of the original spiritual wound yet to be healed.

Below is a description of the effects of the original spiritual wounds. You may notice one or more effects below that describe you. No cause for fear. It's when one or more of these areas become barriers to leading a normal life that thorough healing is required. These barriers may manifest in spiritual areas, social, material or even physical health areas. Besides, you have this book with key principles on healing the wounded spirit, whether major or minor wounds.

Mental Effects from Original Wounds & their Byproducts
- Recurring bad dreams
- Recurring memories of a past hurt
- Prone to memory losses or distorted memories, exaggerating the negatives
- Focused on faults of others and shifting blame
- Easily critical of others
- Difficulty in forgiving some people
- Either extremely overconfident even when heading the wrong way, or on the opposite end extremely pessimistic
- Either obsessed with cleanliness (clean freak) & hygiene, or on the opposite end extremely dirty (skunk (as an adult, not a teenager)).

Emotional Effects from Original Wounds & their Byproducts
- Either exceptionally withdrawn (extreme introversion), or on the opposite end exceptionally outgoing & people pleaser (extreme extroversion)
- Inferiority complex
- Exceptionally fearful, suspicious and distrustful

- Easily controlled by habits and compulsions like alcohol, drugs, food, or television
- Overwhelming feelings of guilt of some harm done (e.g. military personnel returning from war)
- Easily offended and angered - very sensitive
- Difficulty to give and receive love, praise or approval,
- Either overprotective or possessive, or on the opposite end extremely permissive and indulgent.

Effects in the will from Original Wounds & their Byproducts

- Either excessive workaholism, or on the opposite end complete unconcern for work, career or obligations (sluggard, couch potato, leisureholic, lazybones)
- Either excessive perfectionism (picky, fussy), or on the opposite end loose morals and inability to care on doing what's right (chaotic)
- Either extremely cautious to life, or on the opposite end extremely impulsive and reckless, prone to jumping from fire to fire
- Either extremely domineering personality (control freak, planet, godzilla, bridezilla), or the opposite end extremely weak-willed and easily manipulated (doormat or welcome mat, wimp)
- Exceptionally self-centered
- Exceptionally defensive (even where wrong) & easily shifting blame on others
- Either very stubborn & insensitive to correction (bullheaded, brain-dead), or on the opposite end easily influenced (flip-flop, spineless), preferring peace over integrity
- Either extremely self-driven & unhealthily independent, or on the opposite end extremely others-driven & helplessly dependent on others.

Chapter 7:

Personality's Role in Influencing our Spiritual Health

"Whatever is right, whatever is pure...think about such things"

This chapter predominantly uses secular approaches in addressing matters related to our inner makeup. However the principles shared are so crucial in helping each of us understand ourselves and our place in this life. These principles are from the secular academic field of psychology. There is nothing wrong or sinful about the secular academic world in its non-infiltrated context. It is the matters that contradict or undermine the bible that are no, no for us.

If disciplines from the secular academic world were evil then all of us Christians need to go back to the Stone Age type of living. No school, no reading, no technology and tools invented by the secular academic world. The only thing worth returning to in the Stone Age era is our diet and eating habits. Their diet consisted of whole natural foods, free from genetic modifications, commercial production chemicals, unhealthy preservatives, you name it.

It disturbs me to see fellow believers criticize anything that does not have a bible verse to it. With such a narrow minded approach they end up depriving believers from a lot of beneficial and useful principles that do not contain bible verses. The principles may be beneficial to the body of Christ spiritually, socially, materially, or physically.

The first benchmark for allowing matters that the bible does not specifically cover is whether or not the matters contradict or undermine the bible. If they don't contradict or undermine the bible they pass the first test. *"Finally, brothers, whatever is true, whatever is noble, whatever is right, whatever is pure, whatever is lovely, whatever is admirable—if anything is excellent or praiseworthy—think about such things," Philippians 4:8.*

The second benchmark for allowing matters that the bible does not specifically cover is on their level of reward or benefit they bring to our Christian lives spiritually, socially, materially, and physically. If they are very beneficial they pass the second test. *"Everything is permissible"—but not everything is beneficial. "Everything is permissible"—but not everything is constructive,"* 1 Corinthians 10:23.

In relation to healing the wounded spirit and maintaining spiritual health some principles from the field of psychology pass the two tests. It is these principles that I'll be focusing on in this chapter. First it's worth looking at our unique makeup from a biblical perspective.

Understanding our unique makeup from a biblical perspective

Before we were born God already had a purpose for each of us. He predestined each of us to come on this earth. Scripture says we have been *"predestined according to the plan of him who works out everything in conformity with the purpose of his will," Ephesians 1:11.*

So he made us in a particular way to suit the purpose he has us. The parents we were born to were by his design, our sex, physical and personality attributes are not an accident. Each one of us is therefore in God's design. Inside that design God has all the details about his plans for us - the right career/ministry, workmates, the right spouse (or singleness), friends, areas of residence per period, number of children etc. He works out his agenda in his unseen ways.

He does it to even a greater extent for us Christians since we're specifically his children. A wise parent is committed to nurturing his children in the best possible way. God as our heavenly father has the best plans for us his children.

Sometimes we can be anxious or restless about what's ahead of us. This happens when our focus turns away from him and we start focusing on ourselves as determinants of our destiny. The best way to determine our destiny is to entrust our lives into his hands and continue doing our best in areas that we're responsible for. He's responsible for more than our share. God says to every one of us, "I know the plans I have for you, plans to prosper you and not to harm you, and plans to give you hope and a future," Jeremiah 29:11.

There is, therefore, only one reason for every individual's existence; to fulfill God's plan for his life. Outside that, life is meaningless, a mere struggle a veritable wilderness of trials and temptations. No amount of fame, social status, money and power can bring a sense of fulfillment outside God's plans.

In that design God gives us certain abilities or talents. Each one of us is therefore gifted in one area or another whether we know it or not. There's something we find easy to excel in. We also enjoy committing ourselves in that area. We can even volunteer to assist without any reward or work for endless hours without any stress.

Our uniqueness: The Four Temperament Theory

Florence Letterer is gifted in this area of helping people to understand their inborn and learned personality attributes. She has written extensively on this subject. Her most popular book is, "Personality Plus: How to Understand Others by Understanding Yourself". She uses the four temperament personality theory. It is an ancient personality analysis that categorizes people into four types.

Some Christian authors like Tim Lahaye have claimed to trace the theory from the Bible in the book of Proverbs. However, this only served to put Lahaye on the receiving end of a lot of criticism from many in the body of Christ. Tim Lahaye was actually the earliest Christian advocate to resurrect the ancient four temperament personality theory. His book, "Why You Act the Way You Do", became a popular reference in Christian counseling circles. I've read it and find it very informative. It's fun to read too.

It is only where the bible is used to back the theory that there is a problem. It's fitting to categorize bible personalities into personality types. This is not unscriptural. Where it's not fitting is to claim that the theory is from the bible. However this is not a major error compared to many false teachings circulating in the body of Christ. Lahaye received too much criticism on a matter that was blown out of proportion.

The four temperament personality theory is part of personality theories in the secular academic field of psychology. It is among the many personality theories in the field of psychology. It is in the category of "Personality Type" theories of personality. The following is a list of the categories of personality the major theories in the field of psychology:

- Personality Type theories
- Personality Trait theories,
- Behavioral Personality theories
- Cognitive Personality theories
- Psychoanalytic Personality theories
- Humanistic Personality theories
- Biopsychological Personality theories

Personality Type theories classify people into different types of behavioral characteristics. For example the four temperament personality theory classifies people into four different personality types. Another among the Personality Type theories is one that puts people into two types. It is called like the Introversion and Extraversion theory. Other Personality Type theories like the Myers-Briggs Type Indicator (MBTI) have more complex classifications and measures.

Advantages of the four temperament personality theory

The four temperament personality theory has many advantages. It helps in understanding oneself. Understanding yourself is one of the most liberating experiences in your life. It brings awareness about your individuality which helps you appreciate yourself. Instead of wishing to be like someone else who may have a personality you admire you realize you actually have admirable personality traits as well.

You realize that you have a set of admirable strengths while also having unpleasant weaknesses. With that, also comes the realization that it's the same for everyone else out there. There are no perfects. The only perfection is to strive to maximize the expression of your strengths while striving to minimize the expression your weaknesses. As a Christian this is important. Knowing your strengths helps you to cooperate with God in effectively using the natural gifts he has entrusted you with. Knowing your weaknesses helps you to cooperate with God in effectively preventing your weaknesses from hindering you.

It helps in interpersonal relationships and behavior. The principles in the theory help to relate with others in personal, verbal, and emotional circumstances. It is a communication facilitator. By understanding the different makeup of people you're able to relate with others in a better way. For example, if some are detailed oriented and you're not you'll be able to relate with them at their level or at least in a negotiating way rather than being irritated by their "strange" detail needs.

This type of accommodation and understanding of others is helpful in intimate relationships and in other social relationships, like in work or school settings. It can also help in conflict resolution skills. Though not the only guide, a personality self appraisal helps in pointing to some career preferences related to one's personality.

As Christians the Holy Spirit is our primary guide. It is not strange to find the Holy Spirit guiding a person in a career area related to one's personality. For us Christians any career is a ministry. It is a profession through which God is able to use us in being vessels to show his nature through us. This nature being expressed by our conduct, our diligence, our concern for others, and where there is an opportunity our witnessing to others. In addition, it is through our primary areas of ministry (work) that our financial earnings come from. The way we use our financial earnings for the various needs, whether for personal or corporate interests, determines where our hearts are; to the interests of God and fellow humanity or to our own interests.

It helps in understanding oneself in dealing with your emotions. Emotional health is guided by understanding. Although emotions are separate from reason or the mind, they are guided by the mind. Try screaming in a public square if you drop your cell phone. Your mind says it's not appropriate. Whereas when you drop it at home you may yell at the phone, at least some personalities have this tendency.

Having an understanding of your unique self therefore helps in dealing with your emotions. Your mind takes an active role in controlling the various emotions going inside you when you purposely decide or work on your emotions to go toward a desired direction. This is better than yielding to the sometimes irrational whims of emotions.

Understanding your unique self therefore helps in exercising your emotional strengths while minimizing your emotional weaknesses. It gives you a sense of direction rather than mere guesswork. More understanding of yourself helps you gain what some call emotional judgment, emotional intelligence, and emotional health.

Disadvantages of the four temperament personality theory

Its biggest disadvantage is that it's limited. This is what gives fuel to a lot of its critics. However, most academic inquiry is limited. The field of medicine is both art and science (and big money business in our time). Should its limitation be the basis to abandon it? No.

It is very stereotypical. The theory places people into boxes of personality types. In real life we're all very unique in our combination of personality traits and behavior. The only consolation is that the theory states that we're all a unique combination of various levels from any of the four types. It is the support for the unique combination of traits each of us has that makes the theory more acceptable.

The four temperament personality theory

Now that we've covered on the makeup of the four temperament personality theory we can focus on its nature. The theory says each one of us has one major personality type and at least one minor one. The major one is the most dominant that people can easily describe us by. The minor one is the one we know ourselves and people close to us.

The four personality types are:
1) Sanguine;
2) Melancholy;

3) Choleric;
4) Phlegmatic.

Traits of a Sanguine	
Strengths	Weaknesses
Outgoing, Sociable	Undisciplined
Inspires Allegiance	Easily Influenced
Sincere	Restless
Positive Attitude	Disorganized
Responsive to Others	Undependable
Talkative	Loud
Enthusiastic	Promotes Self
Seldom Worries	Exaggerates
Compassionate	Fearful, Insecure
Generous	Unproductive

Traits of a Melancholy	
Strengths	Weaknesses
Natural Talent	Moody
Analytical	Negative
Perfectionist	Critical
Conscientious	Resists Change
Loyal	Self-Conscious
Organized	Unpredictable
Idealistic	Revengeful
Sensitive	Lacks Self Confidence
Self-Sacrificing	Unsociable
Self-Disciplined	Theoretical

Traits of a Choleric	
Strengths	Weaknesses
Determined	Unsympathetic
Independent	Inconsiderate
Productive	Resists Regulations
Decisive	Cruel, Sarcastic
Practical	Doesn't Give Recognition
Goal Oriented	Self Sufficient
Optimistic	Domineering
Willing to Risk	Opinionated
Self Confident	Proud
Willing to Lead	Cunning

Traits of a Phlegmatic	
Strengths	Weaknesses
Calm, Quiet	Unmotivated
Easygoing	Unexcitable
Likeable	Avoids Conflict
Diplomatic	Spectator
Efficient, Organized	Selfish
Dependable, Stable	Stingy
Conservative	Stubborn
Practical	Self-Protective
Reluctant Leader	Indecisive
Dry Humour	Risk of Fear

Our uniqueness: Introversion & Extraversion

This section will cover on the Introversion and Extraversion theory of personality in relation to healing the wounded spirit and maintaining spiritual health.

Each of us, regardless of having or not having wounds has some combination of introversion and extroversion. The degree of introversion or extroversion varies from person to person depending partly on hereditary factors and partly on upbringing factors. No trait is better than another. They complement each other. The extreme flaws or spiritual wound effects of each trait are both as destructive.

Introversion

Introversion is a tendency to be shy, inward drawn and interested in one's thoughts and feelings rather than in other people or external events in the world. People with a high degree of introversion are characterized as introverts. They are said to be shy, quiet, less sociable, sensitive, and cautious, constantly in deep thoughts and minding their own soul-searching business.

Spiritual wounds predisposed to introverts

The extreme flaws that characterize introverts include nervous and mental diseases such as depression, schizophrenia, worry and anxiety disorders, excessive perfectionism, feelings of inadequacy and hopelessness. At their worst level introverts end up under psychological care, in metal hospitals or attempt suicide.

Some introverts may have extreme tendencies that are predominant among and characteristic of extroverts but this is an exception rather than the norm. This could be due to having a high combination of extroversion traits.

Why are introverts more prone than to have spiritual wounds of such nature? Lucinda Bassett, from Midwest Center for Stress and Anxiety says it is because introverts are very analytical. They are natural born thinkers who have a tendency to analyze and ponder on matters spiritual, social, economical and scientific.

This is a natural gift, they have the mental energy and commitment to go an extra mile in using their minds. However, when this energy of thinking and analyzing is turned inward it easily turns into negative energy. The introvert begins to overanalyze matters that everyone goes through and which others do not easily allow to bring their spirits down.

The analytical and introspective traits of introverts can develop into unhealthy tendencies of perfectionism and sensitiveness. Common imperfections and the ups and downs of life can easily break the inner strength of some introverts and cause them to break down. Severe experiences are even more unbearable to those who want everything in life to work perfectly smooth.

By learning to see the world in its fallen state and overcoming the compulsion for perfection introverts nursing a wounded spirit can be able to deal with life's obstacles in a positive way. Healing becomes automatic.

Instead of destructive or negative thinking and analysis a constructive or positive thinking approach to matters in life can lift up one's spirit into a whole new experience of life. It can open new levels of faith, hope, and opportunity that would never have been realized during the time of being preoccupied with the past or any imperfections.

In psychology the tendency toward negative thinking is called call neuroticism. A person with this tendency is referred to as neurotic. Many that are stuck in a cycle of destructive or negative thinking and analysis are actually very intelligent and talented people and don't just don't realize that. Universities and history have a long list of the smartest at some point suffering from mental disorders.

When self-inflicting introverts overcome their destructive approach and cease playing the low self esteem and negativity songs many can find themselves in the most fulfilling careers, positions, outreach work, marriages, you name it. Developing their attitudes and perceptions on life can help them express the many talents they already have. Though many don't even know what they have. A cloud of witnesses in heaven are cheering for them to utilize their gifts and make a difference in this world.

It's often said that our attitude more than our aptitude determines our altitude in life. Our attitude in the spiritual sense is faith in action. *"By faith the people passed through the Red Sea as on dry land; but when the Egyptians tried to do so, they were drowned," Hebrews 11:29.* What would otherwise drown somebody can be a path to success for a person of faith with a positive attitude.

It's also said that, "All the water in the world won't sink a ship - unless it gets inside it." How we react to matters, not necessarily the matters themselves, influences how we will navigate our way forward. The unpleasant water is all around us. Our challenge is to insure it does not get inside our boats of life.

Extroversion

Extroversion is the opposite of introversion. It is a tendency to be self-confident in public, outgoing, social, friendly, and interested in things outside oneself rather than interest in inner feelings or thoughts. People with a high degree of extroversion are characterized as extroverts. They are said to be uninhibited with other people, sociable, friendly, outgoing, impulsive and many times in a jovial mood to please others.

These terms from the secular academic world of psychology are quite simplistic in describing our make-up. However quantitative research has shown the nature of extreme negative flaws that characterize each of the two traits. The extreme flaws are called the weakness tendencies of each trait. In our Christian context we can call them effects of spiritual wounds on each trait.

Spiritual wounds predisposed to extroverts

The extreme negative flaws that characterize extroverts are usually opposite to introverts. They are more outward than inward. They include anti-social behavior, inability to care on doing what's right, violence, aggression, criminal behavior and prostitution to name a few.

Some extroverts may have extreme tendencies that are predominant among and characteristic of introverts but this is an exception rather than the norm. Having such tendencies could be due to having a high combination of introversion traits.

At their worst level of spiritual wounds extroverts end up harming other people, being a problem to society, and in prison if law enforcement agents take action. Needless to say that the human law enforcement system is desperately lacking in enforcing its authority on people that harm others through direct or indirect means such as greed, exploitation, harmful illegal drugs, detrimental and immoral products, services, music, films, etc.

If many of these sinful acts that harm others could be prosecuted and deemed morally unacceptable there would be more people punished for adversely harming others. Many super rich would be among them.

"Now listen, you rich people that amassed wealth inappropriately, weep and wail because of the misery that is coming upon you...Look! The wages you failed to pay the workmen who mowed your fields are crying out against you...You have condemned and murdered innocent men, who were not opposing you," James 5:1, 4, 6.

So the human legal and ethical system has many loopholes. The Lord's spiritual legal system on the other hand is flawless. His word even says he will hold all accountable on Judgment Day.

This includes violators who, without his mercy, walked away scot-free from the human legal system.

In seeking rectification where wronged we, as Christians, have the Lord as our Judge. He knows the outcome of every matter in our lives. In addition, the angels, God's spiritual law enforcement agents, are always ready to enforce his spiritual laws. They are far more thorough in taking action than human law enforcement agents. God ensures that matters intended to work against us are either blocked by his angels or are ultimately made to work to our good.

We're able to seek his intervention with our spiritual weapons of war that are far mightier than human weapons (e.g. arguments, lawsuits, physical confrontation, war). With punishment and vengeance ultimately being in his hands and power he is able to ensure the guilty are punished or mercifully have their eyes opened.

Our uniqueness: Cognitive Personality Theories

Cognitive Personality theories emphasize mental, cognitive or thought aspects of a person as main determinants of personality. They focus on mental or cognitive processes such as thinking, perception, attention, learning, remembering, concept formation, problem solving, and verbal behavior. Cognition is basically the act of using the mind in the various ways that include thinking and perception.

Thus these theories see the mind as a processing system, much like a computer's. For a person to understand himself and his personality, Cognitive Personality theories argue that a person needs to understand his/her mental cognitive processes such as thinking, perception, attention and remembering.

Cognitive Personality theories are the focus in a psychology field known cognitive psychology. Here is a definition of cognitive psychology: *"Cognitive psychology is concerned with information processing, and includes a variety of processes such as attention, perception, learning, and memory. It is also concerned with the structures and representations involved in cognition. The greatest difference between the approaches adopted by cognitive psychologists and by the Behaviorists is that cognitive psychologists are interested in identifying in detail what happens between stimulus and response...The mind has structural and resource limitations, and so should be thought of as a limited capacity processor,"* Michael R.W. Dawson, PhD, "Cognitive Psychology," University of Alberta, Department of Psychology.

Our uniqueness: Behavioral Theories

Behavioral Personality theories, or just Behaviorism, focus on behavior in understanding personality. Instead of looking at unseen mental aspects like cognitive psychology Behavioral Personality theories focus on the observed behaviors of a person to determine their personality. Specifically they focus on the influence of external stimuli or external cause factors on one's behavior.

Thus when using behavioral personality theories to understand yourself, you would want to focus on your behavior in relation to how you react to various external factors. For example, we react differently in a situation of an accident. Some run for protection, others remain on the scene to help people seek protection, others freeze on the scene until someone helps them, some just watch, and still others go on minding their own self-centered business while ignoring what took place. The same incident yet people behave differently and all in varying degrees.

A strategy I may suggest for using behavioral personality theories to understand yourself is to combine it with the four personality temperament theory covered earlier. Knowing your strengths and weaknesses outlined by the four personality theory helps you to monitor behaviors you consider worth changing to move forward. You may then use its conditioning principles for changing behavior. The most noteworthy conditioning mechanism is called Operant Conditioning, which will be covered shortly.

It is this focus on behavior that has made behavioral personality theories popular in secular counseling circles. Counseling using behavioral theories is known as Behavior Therapy. Behavior therapy uses various behavioral principles like reinforcement, rewards and punishments in treating behavioral and emotional difficulties. This process is known as conditioning in the field.

The two main types of conditioning of behavior are Operant Conditioning and Classical Conditioning. Classical Conditioning is sometimes called Pavlovian or Respondent Conditioning. Operant conditioning is the use of consequences to modify the occurrence and form of behavior. Operant conditioning is distinguished from Pavlovian conditioning in that operant conditioning deals with the modification of "voluntary behavior" through the use of consequences, while Pavlovian conditioning deals with the conditioning of behavior so that it occurs under new antecedent conditions. Operant Conditioning in particular can be helpful even for self-treatment of bad habits and unpleasant emotional responses.

"Reinforcement and punishment, the core tools of operant conditioning, are either positive (delivered following a response), or negative (withdrawn following a response). This creates a total of four basic consequences, with the addition of a fifth procedure known as extinction (i.e. no change in consequences following a response).

It's important to note that organisms are not spoken of as being reinforced, punished, or extinguished; it is the response that is reinforced, punished, or extinguished. Additionally, reinforcement, punishment, and extinction are not terms whose use are restricted to the laboratory. Naturally occurring consequences can also be said to reinforce, punish, or extinguish behavior and are not always delivered by people.

- *Reinforcement is a consequence that causes a behavior to occur with greater frequency.*
- *Punishment is a consequence that causes a behavior to occur with less frequency.*
- *Extinction is the lack of any consequence following a response. When a response is inconsequential, producing neither favorable nor unfavorable consequences, it will occur with less frequency.*

Four contexts of operant conditioning: Here the terms "positive" and "negative" are not used in their popular sense, but rather: "positive" refers to addition, and "negative" refers to subtraction. What is added or subtracted may be either reinforcement or punishment. Hence positive punishment is sometimes a confusing term, as it denotes the addition of punishment (such as spanking or an electric shock), a context that may seem very negative in the lay sense. The four procedures are:

1) *Positive reinforcement occurs when a behavior (response) is followed by a favorable stimulus (commonly seen as pleasant) that increases the frequency of that behavior. In the Skinner box experiment, a stimulus such as food or sugar solution can be delivered when the rat engages in a target behavior, such as pressing a lever.*

2) *Negative reinforcement occurs when a behavior (response) is followed by the removal of an aversive stimulus (commonly seen as unpleasant) thereby increasing that behavior's frequency. In the Skinner box experiment, negative reinforcement can be a loud noise continuously sounding inside the rat's cage until it engages in the target behavior,*

*such as pressing a lever, upon which the loud noise is
removed.*

3) *Positive punishment (also called "Punishment by contingent
stimulation") occurs when a behavior (response) is followed
by an aversive stimulus, such as introducing a shock or loud
noise, resulting in a decrease in that behavior.*

4) *Negative punishment (also called "Punishment by contingent
withdrawal") occurs when a behavior (response) is followed
by the removal of a favorable stimulus, such as taking away a
child's toy following an undesired behavior, resulting in a
decrease in that behavior,"* (Wikimedia Foundation, Inc.,
Wikipedia, "Operant Conditioning").

Combined with Cognitive theories, Behavioral Personality
theories make a good team. One focuses on changing the way of
thinking or cognition while the other focusing on changing the
way of behaving.

Cognitive Personality theories are used in combination with
Behavioral Personality theories in counseling by secular
psychiatrists. When combined they become Cognitive Behavioral
Personality theories. Psychiatric counseling using the
combination of cognitive and behavioral personality theories is
known as Cognitive-Behavioral Therapy (CBT). CBT and its
offshoots will be covered in more detail further into this book.

Chapter 8:

Healing the Wounded Spirit: With the Holy Spirit

<u>Avoiding jumping to conclusions on the root causes</u>

Jumping to conclusions is basically guessing and assuming the guessed matter is the true answer to the subject of inquiry. A person reaches such a conclusion due to either;

1) The lack of needed information to make an informed inquiry, or
2) disregarding the need for objective inquiry.

Jumping to conclusions is the opposite of objective inquiry. Objective inquiry considers all available information before making any conclusions. It is a search for the actual truth rather a search to prove one's side of understanding, biases or preferences. There will be more on this subject later.

The most vulnerable areas in life that people tend to be less objective are areas that that do not need to be subject to laboratory or evidenced based inquiry. And what other field is not subject to laboratory or evidenced based inquiry than religion? As religious people we are the masters of making easy conclusions even where objective inquiry can be made.

For example, in USA after New Orleans and neighboring states were badly hit by Hurricane Katrina there were nearly as many answers on its causes as the people you'd come across. It was worse when you heard from ministers, because you expect ministers to be well informed people and more cautious not to make guesswork conclusions. This tendency is among the major factors that have contributed to us ending up having many denominations (and non-denominations) in the body of Christ. The other major factor is as the bible says: we know in part, i.e. we do not have perfect knowledge.

Some people disagreed on certain interpretations ended up forming their own group after being constantly ignored. Some were right in their understanding, like Martin Luther, the protestant church reformer who broke away from the Roman Catholic Church. Others were very wrong in their analysis, like the Jehovah's Witnesses' founder.

Centuries ago we used to fight over our denominational differences or hang those that differed from the dominant denomination. The dissenters or doctrinal rebels in those days used to be called heretics. Now we're more mature and more tolerant of each other, for the most part. We're able to tolerate our somewhat different interpretations and convictions by focusing on the fundamental issues most of us agree on.

Nonetheless there is only one truth. We cannot all be right on one issue with different interpretations, or different misinterpretations. We're all God's children yet what we know or don't know will influence our outcomes in this life. That is why it's not worth being stubborn about holding on to teachings that have been found to be in erring or misinterpretations of scripture.

In this section my emphasis is to be careful to not be jumping to conclusions on the root causes of matters in our spiritual areas. Objective inquiry is essential whether as a Christian counselor, minister, as an intercessor, as a patient, or as a believer helping someone. Objective inquiry for us Christians is what we call biblical inquiry or biblical analysis. With biblical analysis we use the bible by considering all available information before making any conclusions. We search for the actual biblical truth rather searching to prove our own side of understanding, biases or preferences.

This becomes more crucial when dealing with major obstacles others may be facing. Instead of prescribing easy answers we seek sound biblical answers. It also becomes crucial when dealing with matters that partly require our spiritual discernment. This is because our spiritual discernment is not perfect. It can be limited or colored by our own understanding, emotional hunches, and expectations. If you think our spiritual discernment is perfect try taking someone with a spiritual problem to seven different ministers who claim to be so anointed with the gift of discernment. You're likely to get at least two different answers. It won't surprise me even if you get five different answers.

The bible says we're to test the spirits. "Dear friends, do not believe every spirit, but test the spirits to see whether they are from God, because many false prophets have gone out into the world," 1 John 4:1. John was saying that each Christian was liable to receive revelations from various spirits other than the Spirit of God. There are two categories of spirits that are other than the Spirit of God. One category consists of human spirits and the other category consists of evil spirits.

The most important way of testing the spirits behind matters we're analyzing is by using God's word as the standard of evaluation. We use the bible by considering all available information before making any conclusions.

Avoiding easy conclusions when dealing with a Wounded Spirit

There are two ways demons or fallen angels can have access to human beings. These so called loopholes are what enables them to have increased access to affairs in the earthly realm. God in his own design allowed fallen angels to use these avenues:
1) Demonic influence or demonic interference.
2) Demonic possession: a form of demonic indwelling or inner occupancy of demons.

1) Demonic influence or demonic interference

This is external access whereby the evil spirits in the spirit realm are able to access our inner human faculties and our physical makeup. For example, God gave permission to Satan to afflict Job with diseases. His physical body was accessed. He lost his material possessions: His material belongings were accessed. He lost his family: His social life was accessed. The only area that Satan was not given access to was his inner human faculties: his spirit consisting of the mind, will and emotions. None of the experiences of Job were aspects of demon possession. They were aspects of demonic influence or demonic interference.

Someone we know in the bible whose inner human faculties were accessed is Saul, the first king of Israel. In his case it was actually an angel of God that was sent to torment him. God's angels can be sent to cause harm if God wills. Let's not blame every bad matter on demons (fallen angels). Saul had disobeyed God on many occasions. Through his continued disobedience the Lord allowed a tormenting spirit to come upon Saul. "Now the Spirit of the Lord had departed from Saul, and an evil spirit from the Lord tormented him," 1 Samuel 16:14.

David, the person God had secretly chosen to replace Saul as king, comforted Saul by playing music for him. The music from David proved to be good medicine for Saul. "Whenever the spirit from God came upon Saul, David would take his harp and play. Then relief would come to Saul; he would feel better, and the evil spirit would leave him," 1 Samuel 16:23.

The torment Saul experienced was from an external position. In any case God's angels do not possess people. It is fallen angels that do this whenever they can find the opportunity to possess people. His experience was therefore an aspect of angelic influence or angelic interference. I say angelic influence in his case because it was not as a result of fallen angels that we also call demons. Thus in the case of Saul an angel from God was sent to torment him.

Some people, like Saul, may be facing angelic interference in their lives. God specifically assigns one of his angels to interfere in an individual's life in a certain area. It's not that God delights in doing this. There is a cause and effect relationship. Thus something in a person's life led God to have one of his angels to hinder a person. The most common causes are unforgiveness of others, unrepented sins, ignoring the troubles of the underprivileged (spiritually, materially, socially, or physically); and repeated disobedience in areas where God has called for change. Related to Job is Apostle Paul. God allowed Satan to hinder Paul in an area he called his "thorn in the flesh." We may speculate on precisely what this was but it still ends up pointing to the fact that God can give evil spirits to hinder us in areas they have no legal grounds. "There was given me a thorn in my flesh, a messenger of Satan, to torment me," 2 Corinthians 12:7.

Even in such situations where God allows an evil spirit to bring a particular hindrance he does not delight in doing this. There is a good reason God allows it. In Paul's case God wanted to keep him from growing proud from the many exploits God did through him. Paul also ascended through visions to the third heaven and received revelations God said were just for his consumption. His writings constitute a third of the New Testament!

2) Demonic possession

Christians cannot be indwelt, owned or possessed by demons. Christians can be oppressed from an external interference position but not from within. External demonic interference is what constitutes demonic influence as described above. Dealing with demonic influence in relation to severe cases is through the same way all cases of demonic interference are dealt with.

Making easy conclusions and applying false teachings

Christian counseling and deliverance ministry has had its limits and blunders in such a work of piecing together one's entire life and hoping to fix it.

I grieve with anyone who ended up with more wounds after innocently visiting deliverance ministries that apply false doctrine on deliverance. There are heaven destined born again Christians today having a hard time living on earth partly due to spiritual wounds and partly due to having fallen into the wrong hands.

From these deliverance ministries a councilor (usually the church pastor) would listen to a problem and before long begin to identify spirits attacking the victim. Some of the most commonly mention spirits include generational spirits, territorial spirits, spirits of lust, witch spirits, spirits of infirmity, familiar spirits, jezebel spirits, spirits of homosexuality, and spirits of prostitution.

The entire life of a believer is said to be in the hands of one or more of these spirits. Once they are cast out freedom comes. The spirits are ordered to come out but deliverance does not come. Why not?

It is because the evil spirits were not even in the believer in the first place. Demonic influence from an external position was the cause, not demonic possession. Demonic possession is the indwelling of demons. The Christian had a demon influence problem not a demonic possession problem. What may follow in a believer's life is usually one application of false doctrine after another, hoping to find freedom.

But there is a way out for every sincere believer. No need to blame any ministry embracing false doctrine for any further losses you may have faced - spiritually, socially, or materially. Categorize the experience as a storm of life in which God allowed it to occur without choosing to stop it. If he allowed it in your sincere search he knows how to work the entire experience to your good.

The ministries that embrace false doctrines on deliverance are mostly sincere but deceived saints. It is not deliberate misinterpretation of scripture if it's from deceived saints. Explaining why God allows such harmful deception in the body of Christ is another lengthy topic with its own limitations. Our work as Christian counselors in deliverance ministry is to enable wounded believers, most of whom are intelligent people, to effectively connect with the Holy Spirit.

God desires to walk with each of us on a personal, one to one level, not through another human being who assumes to be more spiritual. When this direct relationship is consolidated we're able to effectively deal with matters in our own lives. In the case of a wounded spirit the Holy Spirit will be able to make the matters to work to our good instead of against us. He is also able to show us the key doorways that are allowing the demonic influence, not possession.

Our part in the healing process: Embracing Truth in God's Word

Where do we start in applying the Christ-centered principles that enable the Holy Spirit to bring deliverance and healing to the wounded spirit? We start with the understanding that we have a part to play in the healing process.

Our individual input or role in the healing process is fundamental. A person with spiritual wounds does not have a demonic possession problem. He/she is not owned by some other power. So he's in control of his own core faculties; the mind, emotions, will. It can be a demonic influence problem but hardly for unbelievers, or never for believers, a demonic possession problem.

Demonic influence is something we all face and are divinely empowered, through the Holy Spirit, to overcome. We're in control of our own faculties when it comes to demonic influence. That's why we'll be judged on how we handled demonic influence in our lives; triumphing over it or yielding to it.

For example, in the case of a wounded spirit from a bad past demonic influence comes in the form of evil spirits trying to exalt the bad past above the power of God against it. They tactfully present the unpleasant past to appear hopelessly damaging that an individual is constantly tormented and overpowered by it. This lie that demons present to us is overcome by God's word. The truth frees us from believing the lie. It takes an individual's personal input and inner witness of the Holy Spirit to embrace the truth and forsake the lies. An inner witness of the Holy Spirit is not some voice, even though this can happen, but is very rare.

An inner witness of the Holy Spirit is a conviction from within that God brings, saying some action needs to be taken. There has been enough of making excuses that limit God's ongoing work in each of us. Acknowledging the fact that a problem exists and that it needs to be handled God's way is the first step to overcoming it. Justifying the problem, making excuses, blaming the past or others are barriers to conquering it. The inner witness of the Holy Spirit overcomes these barriers to enable the person to be willing to confront and deal with the matters. It is God's way of bringing the truth and the individual being responsive enough to be able to receive it.

God may use different avenues for different individuals to bring the truth. It may be through qualified spiritual individuals at church or through counseling. It can be a book such this one. It may be through internet resources, audio/visual resources, the list goes on. Whichever way the truth is revealed, the individual's personal input will determine the final outcome. The individual has to be willing enough to labor in doing his/her part of embracing God's way and overcoming the lies that stand in the way. Some may receive instant freedom after embracing the truth, others may take longer while some if they remain in denial for the truth may take forever to heal or recover.

God's Role: The Holy Spirit in the Healing Process

Healing the wounded spirit is primarily the work of the Holy Spirit. Many secular counselors, psychiatrists or psychotherapists have something to offer but a lot has to be integrated with spiritual principles. There is actually much research and information we can benefit from the secular world of psychology and related medical fields.

On the other hand, secular academics have also benefited from the bible by learning most workable principles from the scripture, with little or no acknowledgment to the bible. God's prescription is always the ultimate prescription. Without the integration with spiritual or Christian principles the secular prescription is largely limited in its effect. That is why many under secular treatment are under perpetual care that they fail to stand and deal with matters on their own.

Secular counselors, psychiatrists or psychotherapists are popularly known as shrinks in USA. Its sarcastic meaning descends from an old term "headshrinker." This means a shrink shrinks the brain of a person by disabling him/her from thinking for himself or herself. In extreme cases a person literally ends up under the constant care of a counselor year after year. The word "shrink" now refers to all counselors, secular or Christian. The challenge for those seeking counsel is to find a counselor who does not shrink one's brain but empowers it. By any rate the best counselor is one who connects a person with his/her true Counselor, the Holy Spirit.

"I will ask the Father, and he will give you another Counselor to be with you forever-- the Spirit of truth. The world cannot accept him, because it neither sees him nor knows him. But you know him, for he lives with you and will be in you. I will not leave you as orphans," John 14:16-18.

The Holy Spirit lives inside each of us born again Christians. We are like cared for orphans and not like ones left to struggle on their own against forces more powerful than them. The Holy Spirit has a parental role over us. He is able to bring true healing when we enable him to work in the innermost parts of us. Certain mindsets that evolved throughout our upbringing and through various experiences are transformed into Christ-like nature.

The transformation of our minds directly affects the other areas in our spirits, the emotional and will areas. Only the Holy Spirit knows how to piece together matters of our past and use them to work to our good not against us. Secular counseling cannot enable this. This is also not to say all of us Christian counselors are better than secular counselors. There are some Christian counselors who use false teachings in their counseling or deliverance ministries. These false teachings end up doing as much damage, if not worse, on innocent believers seeking deliverance.

Of major concern are deliverance ministries that easily jump to bind and cast out demons from people who are under demonic influence, not demonic possession. They shrink the brains of innocent believers who seek deliverance by casting out demons that are not in a believer. When the Christian returns home in the same state he/she assumes he could have some powerful demons inside him. Christian shrinks have done the harm by focusing on non-applicable matters. Once these innocent souls finally get to where there is biblical deliverance it can be quite a battle in convincing them that the problem is not demonic possession but demonic influence.

Other battles include moving them away from harmful false teachings innocently adopted through books, multimedia and ministries that preach false doctrine. Some are preoccupied with binding and loosing demons, pleading the blood of Jesus against evil spirits, speaking in so called spiritual warfare tongues, or spiritual warfare prayers against evil spirits. Most of them are very intelligent Christians, yet can still be misled when they seek deliverance out of desperation not biblical truth. The believers can end up with more demonic activity after embracing harmful false teachings.

That is why this book was inspired by the Lord; to enable fellow Christians to avoid deliverance ministries that invite more demonic activity and to equip the body of Christ with biblical principles of Christian deliverance and deliverance ministry. These principles if applied provide the required counsel for biblical deliverance and healing in areas of interest. There is no need of further counseling if one reads and applies the biblical principles in this book. Reading through more than once may help in grasping certain unclear areas. Plus there are more resources online at our websites: JesusWorkMinistry.com and SpiritualWarfareDeliverance.com.

Avoid rushing to any nearest deliverance ministry that tries to cast out demons that are actually operating from outside, not inside. You'll avoid much heartache by following Christ-centered principles instead of demon-centered ones. Christ-centered principles may not have a lot of drama and sensation yet they work.

Prayerfully searching for doorways of access

As we draw near to God and submit to his will we also prayerfully search for doorways that are allowing demonic influence. There is no need to wait for some strange discernment or a supernatural word from God while searching. God may speak in a still small voice in our hearts but this usually comes in the midst of the search, through prayer, his word, a sermon, or a book. Sometimes it comes while just resting, minding your own business. Staying still and hoping God will speak is like transcendental meditation, a non-Christian practice. And guess what? You will always hear something when you "blank" your mind out. This because our minds were created to always be active. What you hear may just be a product of any one of the two sources: your own mind at work or Satan speaking like an angel of light.

It is doubtful if god would want to speak in a moment of "blanking out." This is because he never prescribed it as a way for us to hear from him. God gave us a mind to use and he usually speaks through it. It is not evil to think. The only difference with unbelievers is that we have *"the mind of Christ"* 1 Corinthians 2:16 controlled by the Spirit of God.

After praying to hear from God the next step is to apply your faith of believing that he has answered your prayers. You begin to think and think, read and read, on areas relating to your obstacle. Key matters that need to be effectively dealt with may have come through any of the four doorways:

1) deception,
2) ignorance,
3) sin,
4) storms of life, when responded to in an improper way.

Basic steps of faith to deliverance and healing

The doorways that have been found need to be placed on his mercy seat, through repentance. One can now move to applying the basic steps of faith to deliverance and healing:

1) prayer of repentance for walking outside God's will,
2) ceasing all known association and practice of matters that bring bondage through
    a. deception (false teachings),
    b. through ignorance (lack of knowledge),
    c. through sin, and
    d. through storms of life (particularly when responded to in an improper way),
3) being familiar with and applying biblical requirements in areas were deliverance and healing is sought (most biblical requirements in different areas are covered in this book), and
4) a simple prayer to ask God for continued guidance, equipping and grace in opening one's eyes to true biblical living.

Repentance on matters that came through storms of life is necessary when our response to them was in a sinful way. For example if one had an abusive upbringing and remains bitter about it, the bitterness and anger constitutes unforgiveness. Unforgiveness is a sin. Repentance for being bitter, angry or vengeful begins the healing process.

Prayer and fasting may be necessary on certain matters. We are dealing with spiritual strongholds that have consolidated their make-up in our lives. These are mindsets, emotions and defense mechanisms that have evolved throughout years of our upbringing and through various experiences. They become our identity and demonic influence has reinforced their hold on us. At such a level we become brainwashed whereby we either easily follow the deception or easily stumble to certain sins.

Prayer and fasting is one of, if not, the greatest key to deliverance and healing. It enables the Holy Spirit to effectively work in the innermost parts of us. He is able to overcome certain mindsets, emotions and defense mechanisms that we find difficult to give up or unwilling to let go. He transforms our minds to value his ways than our ways. The transformation of our minds directly affects the other areas in our spirits.

However, he also works on these areas individually until we each have "a spirit of power, of love and of self-discipline," 2 Timothy 1:7.

Power is an aspect of the Holy Spirit's ability to act, love is an emotional aspect of his nature and self-discipline is the will aspect of his nature. He throws away our nature which has no power to act over spiritual influences, he removes the dirt in our emotions while putting love in them and he removes our undisciplined will which fluctuates according to circumstances and other external influences. Above all the Holy Spirit enables us to grow in having "the mind of Christ," 1 Corinthians 2:16 so that we can effectively be under his influence, guidance and nature.

Once a human spirit begins to take on his nature, the healing is in progress. Being under his nature is a lifelong work because the sinful nature in us always tries to return to its former throne. Demonic influence works through the sinful nature. That is how Adam and Eve fell. And that is why the bible cautions us to flee influences and situations that feed on the sinful nature.

People will notice the difference by the time the Holy Spirit reaches an advanced stage in working inside us. We will be producing not fruits from our negative past but the fruit of the Holy Spirit.

"The fruit of the Spirit is love, joy, peace, patience, kindness, goodness, faithfulness, gentleness and self-control. Against such things there is no law. Those who belong to Christ Jesus have crucified the sinful nature with its passions and desires. Since we live by the Spirit, let us keep in step with the Spirit," Galatians 5:22-25.

One who is bearing such fruit in abundance has a healthy spirit. He/she may not be perfect in every way or may not have all she desires yet she is an over comer in the spirit realm. Demonic influence bounces off for as long as the Holy Spirit works in her life.

Chapter 9:

Healing the Wounded Spirit: With Secular Approachs

Mental Health and Anxiety Disorders

The spiritual areas of the mind, emotions and will are referred to as mental health areas in the secular world. Matters dealing with the wounded spirit are classified as anxiety disorders. For example the Anxiety Disorders Association of America (ADAA) groups anxiety disorders in the following categories:

1) generalized anxiety disorders,
2) panic disorders and agoraphobia,
3) obsessive-compulsive disorders,
4) posttraumatic stress disorders,
5) social phobia (social anxiety) and
6) specific phobia.

The study of anxiety disorders is a relatively new science that's still evolving. Caution and personal research is needed in seeking treatment from the secular world to avoid ending up as a failed experimental guinea pig. There are two main types of treatment available for all anxiety disorders:
1) medication, and
2) psychotherapy.

Caution is particularly needed when one is prescribed medication. Medication has more controversy than psychotherapy as will be covered below.

1) Medication (With Lots of Caution)

Medication has, from its onset, had controversies. It has had its fierce opponents like Lynn Henderson, who directs the Shyness

Clinic in California, and Philip Zimbardo, a psychologist at Stanford University. Both of whom believe medication only tries to sweep issues under the carpet and not solve anything.

There are different medications and different psychotherapy treatments for different anxiety disorders. Some treatments have been known to work for another or combination of anxiety disorders while others have been known to have disastrous results. Unique differences of anxiety disorders among individuals have also added to the complexity of treatment for anxiety disorders.

For example there are different kinds of medications that have been used to treat social anxiety disorders. The WebMD lists the following: *"antidepressants, like Paxil; tranquilizers (benzodiazepines), such as Xanax, Librium, Valium, and Ativan; beta-blockers, often used to treat heart conditions, may also be used to minimize certain physical symptoms of anxiety, such as shaking and rapid heartbeat,"* (WebMD, Inc, webmd.com).

The main issue to note about medication is that it can help in the short term. However, in the long term it has the potential of being addictive to the point of not being able to function without it. That is why it has fierce opponents. People can get stuck on medication for years or for life, without dealing with the root causes. Side effects of some medication include drowsiness, dizziness, headaches, nausea, and weight gain. Withdrawal symptoms have been experienced by some when they stop taking medication. Withdrawal symptoms have included severe depression and suicidal thoughts or attempts.

If you are married there is another side effect of some anti-anxiety medication. The most publicized ones are anti-depressants that are known to decrease the sex drive. Some professionals say they do more harm than hindering emotions of sexual desire (libido) and performance. They say anti-depressants can hinder the expression of other healthy emotions, particularly expression of love.

Helen Fisher and J. Anderson Thomson maintain that anti-depressants hinder feelings of passion and love. Fisher an evolutionary anthropologist from Rutgers University and Thomson a psychiatrist from the University of Virginia say this is due to the changes in brain chemistry, on the chemicals that anti-depressants are made to manipulate. Thus while some may resolve depression they may end up hindering the emotions that sustain a long-term relationship: love and passion towards a spouse.

Their work is covered in a chapter of a book titled "Evolutionary Cognitive Neuroscience", edited by Steven Platek et al. The book is by many researchers on different topics.

Not only do a lot of mental health drugs hinder love emotions they may also lead to other harmful emotional and mental delusions. There is a lot debate among alternative health practitioners alleging that mental health drugs cause a lot of people to completely lose touch with reality. This in turn makes them to commit even the worst crimes without even realizing their psychosis; irrational and delusional behavior.

The research done by Fisher and Thomson is not conclusive but so is the field of mental health. The field of mental health is a field that is still in its early stages of development. Anyone seeking mental health assistance for yourself, for your child or for anyone it's recommended to countercheck prescriptions by considering information from several sources. With the advent of the internet it is now possible to obtain a lot of such information much easier and more freely.

I'm on the side of mental health practitioners that caution against psychiatric drugs. As a Christian, knowing that drugs cannot address spiritual matters it's plain and simple that fellow Christians seek spiritual remedies instead. Pharmaceuticals deal with the brain wiring and matters of certain supposed chemical imbalances in the brain. They address the physical aspects of what's going on in the brain. They do not address the spiritual aspects that are the actual causes.

As a result the root problem is never resolved with drugs. Worse still is that they bring side effects that may add more salt to the already existing wounds. These side effects include mental, emotional and physiological reactions. I've seen kids that were growing up well only to be stalled by medications their parents' shrinks advised to treat supposed hyperactivity disorders. Mentally some lost their sharpness, became quite emotionally detached, and physically gained a lot of weight while becoming far less energetic. Anyone can say this was not a fair tradeoff just to make a child less hyper.

Hyperactivity "disorders" are normal signs of a child's character. Some personalities are by nature hyperactive. I'm in this category of people that cannot sit still. Hyperactivity was quite a thorn in the flesh to my family in my teenage years. However being hyper is not a problem in itself. The main problem is when the endless energy is diverted to negative matters.

Thus the solution is to work on ensuring such energy is diverted towards positive matters. One of the most negative devices today on children is the secular multimedia world. These include most secular or mainstream television shows, movies and music.

There is nothing as draining and stressful as looking after a hyperactive child who's working to live the lifestyle and behavior he/she is learning from the secular world. All that energy gets thrown into chasing after wind, and even worse, into looking for trouble. I've been one such child, but thanks be to God for his rescue before any disaster happened. The prayers of family members worked to prevent this. But I can imagine many children out there without such a prayer covering.

It takes more work nurturing hyperactive children but it's the rewards ahead, the child's future, that are worth today's input. This is not easy in an era where many parents have time constraints to spend with their children. Sometimes it may be worth cutting one's material needs and pursuits by adjusting to only essentials. Benjamin Franklin once said, "There are two ways to increase your wealth. Increase your means or decrease your wants."

In the Western world we've set the bar of what's "enough" so high it's only working to serve the interests of the big business groups. Many people are literally in a relentless rat-race to increase their means or loading themselves with whatever latest toys of the day. As Christians we can't afford falling into the same trap. Assuming that the grass is greener with abundant joy, happiness, peace of mind, security, and respect by being wealthy is a deception ruining lives of many.

In regard to hyperactive behavior when the energy is directed towards negative matters there is also a dietary component to it. Certain foods magnify hyperactivity to gigantic levels. The biggest culprit is foods with a lot of sugar. Sugar is like alcohol to children. Unfortunately the food industry only works to worsen the problem through their advertising of sugar laden foods to children.

Many schools are flooded with vending machines selling candy (sweets), soda (soft drinks), and other high sugar and calorie laden foods. This has only contributed to higher hyperactivity behavior and a rise in obesity among children. Even "energy drinks" are being advertised to kids. What on earth does a child need an energy drink for?

Such matters in society are why I keep sounding the alarm that we ought to guard ourselves from predators out there that do not have our primary interests. These predators work in the least obvious ways and if we're ignorant of their ways they end up ruining our families, relationships, physical health and more. *"My people are destroyed from lack of knowledge,"* Hosea 4:6.

In the era we live in these secrete predators are not just some greedy business people seeking to profit from anything. We're in a period that the occult world, from a Satanic group the bible calls Mystery Babylon, is busy doing Satan's work. With Satan's time being short he's on a mission to take as many as possible with him and to destroy God's people as much as possible.

2) Psychotherapy (Has its Limitations)

Psychotherapy has more advocates than medication. However both psychotherapy and medication can easily be used in combination by mental health professionals. Psychotherapy involves talking with a trained mental health professional, such as a psychiatrist, psychologist, social worker, or counselor to learn how to deal with problems like anxiety disorders.

Advocates for psychotherapy, like Thomas A. Richards, argue that psychotherapy has the best approach to solving anxiety disorders. A term was born in the 1980s to define the psychotherapy treatment method for anxiety disorders. It is known as cognitive-behavioral therapy (CBT). CBT is basically a combination of cognitive and behavioral theories, covered earlier, used to deal with mental health disorders.

The major aim of CBT is to reduce anxiety by eliminating beliefs, mental associations and behaviors that bring about the anxiety disorder. Cognitive-behavioral therapy, as its name suggests, has two parts:

1) the cognitive component and
2) the behavioral component.
3)

The National Institute of Mental Health (NIMH) says the cognitive component helps people change thinking patterns that keep them from overcoming their fears. For example, a person with a social anxiety disorder might be helped to overcome the belief that others are continually watching and harshly judging him or her.

The behavioral component of CBT seeks to change people's reactions to anxiety-provoking situations. A key element of this component is exposure, in which people confront the things they fear.

For example, a person with social anxiety may be encouraged to spend time in feared social situations without giving in to the temptation to flee. In some cases the individual will be asked to deliberately make what appears to be slight social blunders and observe other people's reactions; if they are not as harsh as expected, the person's social anxiety may begin to fade.

Some people who have successfully conquered mental health disorder, such as their fears, through cognitive-behavioral therapy (CBT) can experience a relapse after long periods of success. The NIMH says that, "*Recurrences can be treated effectively, just like an initial episode. In fact, the skills you learned in dealing with the initial episode can be helpful in coping with a setback,*" (National Institute of Mental Health (NIMH), a branch the National Institutes of Health (NIH), at nimh.nih.gov).

CBT has its offspring or offshoots among professionals who have modified the principles to the point of creating different approaches. A notable one is known as Solution-Oriented Brief Therapy (SBT) or Solution Focused Psychotherapy. Its approach is less past or problem-centered and more solution-centered, a process which is more effective, brief and more empowering. Michele Weiner-Davis is a proponent of SBT, an approach that she uses to help people overcome their obstacles on their own rather than relying on so called "experts" for constant care. She believes professionals like her are meant to empower clients to solve their own obstacles rather than dump matters on counselors to solve them.

In her audio book, "Fire Your Shrink", Weiner-Davis says, "The countless people, who have triumphed over physical illness, poverty, abuse, loss, and emotional devastation, are true experts. Let's learn from them, instead of obsessing over humanity's dark side then running to professionals in the hope that they can cure what ails us.

The idea that "experts" don't have all the answers may not win any popularity contest. A tremendous amount of security is derived in believing in "experts." But it's a false sense of security that in no way compares to the strength you get from knowing that you can depend on yourself.

Since I'm one of those so called "experts" I realize that it may seem somewhat paradoxical for me to tell you to take expert advice off its pedestal, but it's not paradoxical at all... My goal is to put the self back in self-help," Weiner-Davis, "Fire Your Shrink".

Weiner-Davis' book and audio book can be purchased online at her website, DivorceBusting.com. The website is more than about "divorce busting," that is why she has books such as "Fire Your Shrink". Click on the top link "Divorce Busting Store," then on the left link "Audio CDs and Tapes." The book version of "Fire Your Shrink" has been renamed to "Change Your Life and Everyone in It".

About the book and audio book, her website says, "The truth is, as Michele Weiner-Davis discovered when she set out to practice psychotherapy, you don't have to go on a psycho-archaeology expedition to solve your problems.

Exploring your childhood doesn't help you to escape the stranglehold of the past. Knowing why you behave destructively doesn't stop you from overeating or overreacting, curb depression or panic attacks, or build healthy, happy relationships. Even worse, continually thinking and talking about problems makes you feel hopeless.

Determined to find a better way, Michele developed a radically different approach, based on the principles of Solution-oriented Brief Therapy (SBT). Suddenly she was witnessing spectacular triumphs. People who had been stuck for years turned their lives around within days. The transformations were real, immediate, and lasting.

Drawing on more than a decade of experience with individuals, couples, and families, Michele explains:

- *why looking to the past for understanding prolongs the problem*
- *how to find "the expert within" and break free of unproductive ways of thinking, feeling, and acting*
- *how to translate overwhelming problems into achievable goals*
- *how, despite what you've been told, you can change other people as well as yourself."*

Other recommended secular professionals include, Lucinda Bassett, from Midwest Center for Stress and Anxiety. She has a self-help, drug free program called Attacking Anxiety & Depression. Her material is more expensive compared to Weiner-

Davis' $10.00 for her audio book. Her approach is similar to that of Weiner-Davis, focusing on empowering people rather than shrinking their brains.

The Limits of Secular Approaches

Healing the wounded spirit is not just a cognitive, mental or brain chemistry issue. It is beyond that. It is a spiritual matter. It this spiritual nature of our inner makeup that the secular world finds itself limited to dealing with. A wounded spirit is a result various matters depending on the doorway the matters entered into a person's life. The four doorways of access were covered earlier.

From the original causes of a wounded spirit there can also be offshoots or other matters that may have added to the problem. For example, someone dealing with matters from the distant past may also be dealing with recent afflictions he/she may be going through. The person's personality makeup may also be facilitating the problem, particularly when a person does not know his/her areas of weakness and vulnerability.

Thus to precisely identify the root causes from thousands or even millions of experiences in life is not humanly possible. Only the Holy Spirit whose knowledge is infinite knows how to take care of such a puzzle. That is why secular psychology and related fields of study are limited. Much has been unearthed through these noble fields. But they cannot replace a responsibility that is primarily spiritual in nature.

How else can we explain former prisoners, drug addicts, prostitutes, homosexuals, victims of abuse, emotional wretches, and others being more likely to change and receive deliverance through God's word than through all the secular counseling they could get?

Chapter 10:

Breaking The Strongholds Hiding in Our Lives

Reality: the state of things as they truly are, no biases

This is an extension of the topic on Cognitive Theories covered in Chapter 7: Personality's Role in Influencing our Spiritual Health. Cognition is basically the act of using the mind. Various mental processes in the course of using the mind include thinking, perception, attention, learning, remembering, concept formation, problem solving, verbal behavior, etc. The chapter will focus on mental flaws or mental errors known as cognitive biases that obstruct our thinking processes from seeing things as clearly as they are. They limit us from seeing things as they truly are in reality.

Reality is the state of matters in life as they truly are, rather than as we might assume them to be. The reality being focused on is the qualitative or philosophical reality which cannot be concretely measured or determined in absolute terms. This type of reality is in the category of academics known as social sciences. This is in contrast to quantitative reality which can be concretely measured or determined in absolute terms. 1+1=2 is quantitative reality. It's in the category of academics known as pure or natural sciences.

However quantitative reality has qualitative aspects in many areas. For example, some researchers claim the world is millions of years while others say it is in the thousands. Each endeavors to use quantitative methods of analysis. However because the methods of analysis and measurement have a human element in them they end up being partly qualitative. Qualitative reality is vulnerable to our own biases. It's important to note that many fields in qualitative reality category endeavor to use quantitative methods of analysis to minimize bias. For example, economists have numerous statistical measurements for economies and the world of commerce. The challenge therefore is in minimizing biases so that reality is seen in its truest sense.

Even where it's not practical to devise quantitative methods of analysis it's worth endeavoring to be as objective as possible in making an inquiry and drawing a conclusion. Our area of faith as Christians is one area that can use such inquiry. It helps us to minimize or avoid adding our own biases. Our mental biases, mental errors, or mental flaws, as will be covered shortly, are among the major reasons we have numerous denominations today.

False teachings too, have an element of descending from mental flaws among believers in the body of Christ. It's also our mental biases that can contribute to unnecessary spiritual wounds, strongholds, and other unpleasant matters in this life.

Cognitive Biases: How we Think Inside our Boxes

Instead of seeing reality in its best possible true sense our mental flaws process reality through a filtered method that ends up seeing reality from a biased view. A biased view is a perspective that sees something from our own preference, opinion, or favored outlook with little or no consideration to analyze the facts.

Our biased view on matters in life constitutes our man-made boxes that limit us from seeing reality in its best possible true sense. Our thinking is limited within these boxes that we put ourselves in. They can be either self-made boxes or can be boxes made by others who have successfully put us in a box of their biased views.

Biases are therefore the opposite of objectivity. Objectivity is an independent or neutral analysis that is free from influence of bias.

Objectivity considers all available information without taking any sides. It is a search for the actual truth rather a search to prove one's side of understanding, biases, cultural influences, expectations, or preferences.

To further elaborate on what biases are it is worth giving some examples. Wikipedia, an online Encyclopedia, has a good compilation on biases. Below is a short list of social biases. Social biases are among other forms of cognitive biases.

- *Class bias: bias favoring one social class and bias ignoring social or class divisions;*
- *Commercial bias: advertising, coverage of political campaigns favoring corporate interests, or reporting favoring media owner interests;*
- *Ethnic or racial bias: racism, nationalism, regionalism and tribalism;*
- *Geographical bias: describing a dispute as it is conducted in one country, when the dispute is framed differently elsewhere;*
- *Nationalistic bias: favoring or opposing the interests or views of a particular nation;*
- *Gender bias: including sexism and heteronormativity;*
- *Linguistic bias, favoring certain languages;*
- *Political bias: bias in favor of or against a particular political party, philosophy, policy or candidate;*
- *Religious bias: bias for or against religion, faith or beliefs;*
- *Sensationalist bias: favoring the exceptional over the ordinary. This includes emphasizing, distorting, or fabricating exceptional news to boost commercial ratings;*
- *Scientific bias (including anti-scientific and scientific skepticism): favoring (or disfavoring) a scientist, inventor, or theory for non-scientific reasons. This can also include excessive favoring (or disfavoring) prevalent scientific opinion if in doing so, notable viewpoints are no longer being treated neutrally.*

(Wikimedia Foundation, Inc., Wikipedia, "Bias")

It can therefore be said that bias is the art of interpreting reality with our own feelings, beliefs, preferences, experiences, personalities, and emotions. It is clouding reality with our own subjective perceptions. Objectivity is the art of separating our own feelings, beliefs, preferences, experiences, personalities, and emotions from reality.

Reality as each of us knows it is quite subjective rather than objective in many areas. We largely live in our own boxes, shaped by our inborn makeup (inborn personality traits) and by our upbringing (home, friends, community, education, economics, politics, religion, media, pivotal life experiences, etc). William Hazlitt said, *"We are all of us, more or less, the slaves of opinion,"* (Hazlitt (1778-1830) British essayist).

The result is seeing reality with what cognitive psychologists call "cognitive biases." It is partial realty and partial subjective perception. The percentage of each subject area varies from person to person and from each one's learning curve in life.

What are cognitive biases?

A good definition of cognitive biases is given by Richards J. Heuer, Jr. in his book "Psychology of Intelligence Analysis". His book was apparently written for the Central Intelligence Agency (CIA) for its Center for the Study of Intelligence. If you have no clue who or what the CIA is it may be better to remain clueless. It's certainly not a Christian institution and is capable of doing some "scary" things.

Here's Heuer's definition: "Cognitive biases are mental errors caused by our simplified information processing strategies. It is important to distinguish cognitive biases from other forms of bias, such as cultural bias, organizational bias, or bias that results from one's own self-interest. In other words, a cognitive bias does not result from any emotional or intellectual predisposition toward a certain judgment, but rather from subconscious mental procedures for processing information. A cognitive bias is a mental error that is consistent and predictable." (Richards J. Heuer, Jr, "Psychology of Intelligence Analysis", page 111).

Thus some of what we think is right could be wrong. Each of us can find out if we're willing to test the assumed truth against other different and disagreeing points of view. Thus the challenge is removing subjective perceptions that are blocking the true realty being seen.

It is worth removing the boxes that lock us in our own world of reality because true reality is liberating. Boxes are mental prisons and their harm in life depends on the relative importance of an area they're affecting in our lives. The different kinds of mental boxes are the types of wrong beliefs and perceptions being followed. There are some wrong beliefs and perceptions that are very destructive to one's life while others may not be so harmful.

Like ignorance our mental boxes are a form of mental slavery that render us to be vulnerable to exploitation in the areas of wrong thoughts, beliefs and perceptions. Mental boxes constitute a lack of knowledge to the right understanding. Lack of knowledge is basically ignorance. The bible has sad news about lack of knowledge. *"My people are destroyed from lack of knowledge,"* *Hosea 4:6.*

Lack of knowledge therefore leads to destruction. This destruction can be in any area of one's life: spiritual, social, physical, or material. One of these forms of destruction concerns our spiritual makeup. God's people, not those whose father is the devil (*John 8:44*) are destroyed from lack of knowledge.

God's people are destroyed not because Satan is strong and furious. It is because they lack knowledge in areas Satan, his fellow fallen angels, and malicious people are able to gain access.

Once knowledge in the area of concern is acquired the exploitations a Christian struggled with come to an end. The needed knowledge and understanding in the area of concern brings freedom.

"You will know the truth, and the truth will set you free," John 8:32.

The Christian Box, the only mental box worth remaining in

As Christians the only leash or chain around our necks to keep us from going further is the Christian box. We remain within our box of Christian beliefs even when looking at other beliefs. We have plenty of different interpretations of the bible anyway to examine among ourselves.

It's very healthy examining these other interpretations within the body of Christ. It helps in removing unnecessary denominational boxes. Unnecessary denominational boxes only work to divide us and thus reducing the effectiveness that would come from our combined effort. For example, if I were a Baptist I can freely explore the doctrines and biblical understanding of other denominations on a particular matter. I explore them without a boxed up or preconceived opinion about their understanding. Neither do I keep a preconceived opinion about my church's understanding.

I objectively compare the doctrines and biblical understanding of the two denominations on a particular matter. I ensure that the conclusion to be made will not be influenced by my own preconceptions, feelings, beliefs of my church, preferences, experiences, personality, and emotions. It will be based on objective analysis of biblical interpretations on particular areas. Until finding a satisfactory biblical understanding I keep moving to explore the doctrines and biblical understanding from other denominations (and non- denominations) within the Christian box.

The areas of inquiry may be on teachings on spiritual warfare, deliverance, spiritual healing, tongues, finances, angels, salvation, etc. My understanding is also based on sound doctrinal and biblical analysis within the extensive Christian box rather than merely from the denomination of my affiliation. I feel at liberty to differ with certain doctrinal beliefs within my denomination yet comfortably remain a part of it. It is the major areas of agreement that keep me within the denomination of my affiliation, not just mere acceptance of everything they teach. I strive to be an informed advocate of the Christian faith while avoiding to be a blind loyalist to unnecessary denominational boxes.

I also feel at liberty to associate with fellow believers from other denominations (and non-denominations). I refrain from judging their walk with God simply based on the denomination they belong to. Together we constitute the body of Christ. We're one giant Christian box. It's not perfect but it's functional and doing its work. It will be made perfect when Christ returns.

Removing Unnecessary Boxes: Overcoming the Enemy Within

"You will know the truth, and the truth will set you free," John 8:32.

This is a profound statement from Jesus. It's a groundbreaking and revolutionary statement. It's worth looking at its context. In the NIV bible the passage is titled "The Children of Abraham."

Here is the main part of the short passage. If you read the whole passage from verse 31 to the end of the chapter you'll fall of your chair laughing. The Jews, Jesus' fellow people, were very stubborn to Jesus' teachings. I don't blame them because his teachings were too much to bear. Most of what he said only started making sense after he died, resurrected, and ascended.

"To the Jews who had believed him, Jesus said, "If you hold to my teaching, you are really my disciples. 32Then you will know the truth, and the truth will set you free". 33They answered him, "We are Abraham's descendants and have never been slaves of anyone. How can you say that we shall be set free?" 34Jesus replied, "I tell you the truth, everyone who sins is a slave to sin. 35Now a slave has no permanent place in the family, but a son belongs to it forever. 36So if the Son sets you free, you will be free indeed. 37I know you are Abraham's descendants. Yet you are ready to kill me, because you have no room for my word. 38I am telling you what I have seen in the Father's presence, and you do what you have heard from your father." John 8:31-38.

This is a passage about freedom versus bondage, truth versus deception, genuine versus counterfeit. The Jews, particularly the religious leaders, thought their Jewish biological identity was all that was required to make them God's children. Jesus challenged his own people by stating that they were wrong. They were living a lie and he came to set them free from that lie.

The truths he shared with them were intended to bring freedom to them. He was the one to take them out of their self-made box of traditions which they assumed were fitting. He was sent to set the Jews and every other ethnic group in this world free. His freedom of humanity is primarily centered on deliverance from spiritual and religious bondage or boxes.

Religious people have a way of assuming they have it all together. Try witnessing to Muslim Imams. You're likely to receive lengthy lectures about Islam's rightness you'll find yourself looking at your watch wondering how long the lecture will last. Their spiritual blindness makes them not see the truth. This makes them believe the lies they've received as if they are pure truths.

Jesus' scenario with the religious leaders and the scenario of Muslim Imams happens in the body of Christ as well. Each of us ought to watch for such areas to avoid clinging to beliefs that have no sound biblical basis. They may look as if they do but a deeper inquiry shows their falsehood. They are mere boxes keeping us away from walking out into the truth.

It takes a lot of our input to ensure such boxes are removed from us. Our Christian identity is not all that matters in this life. While we're still here on earth we have a life to live, a Christian journey to travel, battles to win, trials to overcome, storms to weather, and areas of ignorance to replace with understanding.

None of these will be attained just by wearing a badge "I'm a Christian." It takes seeking, work, persistence, and inner strength. These are the areas that are part of our input. God has his role of giving us the grace to do our part. We take over from that point and sweat it out.

It takes our entire inner spiritual makeup to be involved while powered by God's grace through the Holy Spirit. Our minds diligently apply the mind of Christ, our emotions produce the faith, and our will produces self-control, the needed fruits of the Holy Spirit, to keep us focused on what matters most.

"We have the mind of Christ," 1 Corinthians 2:16.

"The fruit of the Spirit is love, joy, peace, patience, kindness, goodness, faithfulness, gentleness and self-control," Galatians 5:22-23.

I have resolved never to accept matters in my Christian faith just because they feel good or simply because they are followed by my affiliated evangelical denomination. This is blind faith. It's not healthy. I have to know the truth on why I believe in something. I've been fooled not once but twice for just accepting matters because they were what my church or denomination taught.

You probably know the old saying, "Fool me once, shame on you. Fool me twice, shame on me." It was shame on me the second time. I didn't take the first wakeup call to ask questions and find answers on matters that were accepted without question.

Opinions, feelings, false beliefs, preferences, personality inclinations, fitting in, and emotions are not the truth. They are subjective perceptions. They are a good start for a Christian when accepting Christianity but only in the beginning as spiritual infants.

When we're newly born-again and embrace Christianity our feelings or emotions dominate. Later on we're to graduate and grow into informed Christians. Otherwise we'll be tossed from here to there by every Christian fad or trend that comes along.

"The body of Christ may be built up until we all reach unity in the faith and in the knowledge of the Son of God and become mature, attaining to the whole measure of the fullness of Christ. Then we will no longer be infants, tossed back and forth by the waves, and blown here and there by every wind of teaching and by the cunning and craftiness of men in their deceitful scheming," Ephesians 4:12-14.

Our biggest enemy is therefore not Satan. It is each of us as individuals. We have to deal with our selves. Remember on Judgment Day there will be no excuse to blame matters on Satan. Adam and Eve tried it and it didn't work. God says we have to take 100% responsibility for our lives. He has given us the power of choice to choose between good and evil, blessings and curses, life and death, understanding and ignorance, faith and fear, forgiveness and resentment (un-forgiveness).

"This day I call heaven and earth as witnesses against you that I have set before you life and death, blessings and curses. Now choose life, so that you and your children may live," Deuteronomy 30:19.

Satan and his fallen angels only try to influence us to choose the wrong sides. They do not control what we ultimately choose after they present their deceptive offers. We are in charge of our own lives. If we decide to take the wrong choices we're our worst enemy. If we decide to make the right choices we are our best asset.

o step out of being enemies to ourselves we start dealing with the enemy within. We start investigating our spiritual makeup of our patterns of thinking, our emotional patterns, and our willpower drive in focusing on certain matters. We therefore start investigating our inner spiritual makeup. We then start to work on the areas we identify as dysfunctional, as weaknesses, as self-destructive tendencies, as internal strongholds, as detrimental boxes, or as spiritual strongholds.

The enemy within each of us should be a concern more than external enemies. External enemies are negative or hostile forces other than us. They are external factors. External enemies we deal with in life include in the earthly realm:

1) some people who may not treat us well,
2) certain circumstances at odds against us, and
3) time.

Time is both a friend and an enemy of our limited existence on earth. In the spirit realm there is Satan and his fellow fallen angels. All these put together comprise external forces endeavoring to work against us. However if our internal makeup is spiritually well grounded none of the external forces can hinder us. The only area they may succeed in hindering us, is in the area

~ 114 ~

God allows. Beyond the permitted area of hindrance they can never be a barrier against us. The rest of the areas that God has given into our hands are therefore determined by our internal makeup and not by the external. The negative external factors keep losing their ground against us as we work on consolidating what it takes internally to overcome them.

We've many biblical and historical examples of people who overcame major external obstacles due to having a well grounded inner makeup. God is able to do the same through us if we're able to cooperate with him in ensuring our self-made inner obstacles are eliminated.

Chapter 11:

Maintaining a Healthy Spirit & Embracing God's "Plan B"

Maintaining a healthy spirit in life's journey

Maintaining a healthy spirit and embracing God's "plan B" is a lifelong exercise and challenge. There are no stops. A believer can graduate from one level of spiritual health and healing to another only to fall down and suffer some spiritual wounds. God forbid that any of us ever experiences any other spiritual injuries.

Maintaining a healthy spirit comes through avoiding matters that can bring spiritual injury thus result in a wounded spirit. It comes through avoiding matters that Satan can use as legal access into our lives. His legal access comes through any of the spiritual doorways covered in this book. These are through:
1) deception,
2) ignorance,
3) sin, and
4) storms of life (when responded to in an improper way).

Avoiding matters that give access to Satan does not come by shear personal determination. It's not by personal might, nor guts, nor power. The bible is clear on this. It comes through our intimate walk with God. This enables the Holy Spirit to effectively live in us, his temples, and overcome anything contrary to his nature. Through the Holy Spirit we are enabled to know "*all truth*" (*John 16:13*) in required areas that Satan seeks to gain access through.

He also enables us to look at sin the way it really is. We're able to see sin as a fake coating of honey containing nothing but poison that is harmful to us spiritually, socially, materially and physically. Temptation may come but his inner voice will enable us not to succumb to it.

As for storms of life the Holy Spirit uses them as assets to work to our good. Instead of being assets that Satan would like to use to block us from moving forward, the Holy Spirit closes his access. God allows storms of life to happen but does not plot them against us. He only does not stop them.

If God allows them to come our way, as bad as they may be, he surely has plan B to ensure whatever happened eventually benefits us.

Embracing God's "Plan B" in life's journey

God's "plan B"" is anything good he can fulfill out of whatever negative matters we may experience in life. Instead of Satan bringing destruction upon us God frustrates Satan's plans and fulfills the unimaginable out of them. In whatever negative matter of our past or about us God is able to turn it around to work to our good. This includes matters we may be carrying as a result of past sins (e.g. a child out of wedlock), matters from deception and from ignorance.

A couple married outside God's perfect will can have a fulfilling marriage to the same level as those married in his perfect will. His only desire is that we be submissive and obedient to him all the remaining days of our lives. Then he'll proceed to work all things (good and evil, past and present, successes and failures, strengths and weaknesses, abilities and disabilities) to our good.

"We know that in everything God works for good with those who love him, who are called according to his purpose," (*Romans 8:28*).

Hallelujah, Praise the Lord!!

That means, as God's children, nothing negative from our past has any negative influence over our lives. God is able to change all past negative circumstances and experiences to have a positive effect on our lives.

As we submit to God and allow him to fulfill his unchanging plans for our lives he is able use all matters in our lives to our advantage. Instead mourning over the past the Lord works things out to the point where we can say like Joseph, *"You intended to harm me, but God intended it for good," Genesis 50:20.*

The past experiences, our disadvantages, circumstances, Satan and his fallen angels, people with ill motives, or whatever cause may have intended to harm us; God is sovereign power and might, who is above circumstances, limitations, impossibilities, closed doors, malicious people, and above Satan.

He is able to transform the negative matters to end up working to our good. Instead of becoming prisons for our lives, caging us in from moving forward, God uses them as stepping stones to our palace for bearing much fruit for God's glory.

Think of Joseph, the man who later told his bad brothers, *"You intended to harm me, but God intended it for good," Genesis 50:20.* It's nice to read the story but imagine yourself in his shoes. You get sold as a slave, stripped off all your human dignity. All the lovely dreams of royalty vanished, your childhood robbed, family bond robbed, and anything else you would want to live for. You know there is a mighty God out there but what have you done to find yourself in this? Nothing.

Maybe you gain some hope that somehow this God will rescue you. So you keep going faithfully serving in your slavery. Then more strange events happen. You're accused of attempting to rape a wife of a high ranking governor. It's all over the media. You're further reduced from a slave to an animal that lives on instinctive drives rather than reason. Could this God have forsaken you? Can anything get worse than this? I've worked jobs where a lot of cash is handled and the mere suspicion that I was pilfering made me want to quit. Being thought of as a thief was hurting enough to bring distress. What more an accusation Joseph got?

We seem to have a lot of easy answers on how Joseph coped with the severe storms that befell him. But the whole truth is that God kept him in the midst of it all. Joseph did not have some high determination and guts to continue trusting in God. He was as frail as any of us. And he had no bible to read on the faithfulness of God. Put in his shoes many of us would rather be dead. Yet God in his power is able to sustain us if we go through the worst of experiences.

When we get out we even wonder how we came out alive, sane and still Christians. It's unfortunate when some depart from the faith or end up in sin or compromise that brings more bondage. This is another side of the story, but glory is to God for those of us who came out alive and Christian.

May he use us to save others that can be vulnerable to Satan's schemes during storms. No one deserves to face destruction, especially after becoming a Christian. May God use us to stand in the gap and allow him to frustrate Satan's attempts while fulfilling his plan B.

Through God all things are possible, bearable, and can be overcome. Unlike Joseph we have the bible to encourage us. With God's word richly living in us the Holy Spirit is able to effectively use it when storms come. He enables us to effectively respond to storms in a way that blocks Satan from using them to work against us.

During my worst trial or is it worst experience of reaping from ignorance, I concluded the best option was dying. Not through suicide but asking God to take my life. I cried almost daily seeking to be in heaven rather than stuck in this weird world. Seeing that death never came I kept praying and fasting for God to do something about it if I was to be of any use here on earth. He did, eventually, after six torturous months.

Between the trial (and reaping to ignorance in my case) and the breakthrough Satan had no room of using the experience to bring destruction. God took over and kept working out plan B on matters he never orchestrated. He probably tells his angels, "Satan can try whatever he wants but I can still use any situation for good."

God used it to reveal the false teachings on spiritual warfare and deliverance, inspired all these books, brought the call into deliverance ministry, and many other matters that cannot be quantified. For anyone in a storm please forget not the discipline of prayer and fasting. Fasting is a powerful weapon in the realm of the spirit. It enables God to fight for us and work on "plan B."

Storms of life do not spell doom for us for as long as our response is in a way that blocks Satan from using them against us. Whether from past or current experiences God can still use them to work to our good. He did it for Joseph, for Jesus, the early disciples and many saints of God throughout history. Why not for us? Yes he still does today. He's the same God who changeth not (*James 1:17*).

Storms of life are unpleasant experiences that befall us out of no fault of our own. These include experiences of:

1) betrayal by a loved one; trusted person, or leader;
2) death of a loved one;
3) experiences of severe physical or emotional abuse;
4) living under a heavily controlled disciplinary environment that brings fear;

5) living under constant negative and critical words;
6) living under rejection;
7) false accusations;
8) terrible divorce experience, as the victim;
9) traumatic experience(s), (e.g. surviving the September 11 terror experience (in Kenya, Tanzania, and USA);
10) traumatic accident, (e.g. casualty of war);
11) having a physical or social disability;
12) having a certain physical appearance society "persecutes;"
13) severe racial, gender and ethnic discrimination or abuse;
14) falling victim to false teachings;
15) genuine trials of faith.

A victim of whatever storm of life ought to focus on God's power, sovereignty and love in fulfilling "plan B."

For instance, one can say to himself/herself, "Satan may have created this mess but God who is more powerful knows how to use it to bring out the best for his glory." Not saying it out of arrogance but out of humility of being God's child. He is the God who fights our battles. God will make a way, where there seems to be no way. Most of us know the song.

Another may say to himself/herself, "It was not a mistake to be born in family Y or living with guardian(s) Y. Neither was it a mistake to be born or living in location Z."

"I am not a mistake, regardless of how, where or when I was born, my appearance, gender, race, tongue, having certain strengths, having certain weaknesses, abilities, disabilities etc. God *"fearfully and wonderfully,"* (*Psalms 139:14*) put all these ingredients together for a particular purpose.

"I may not understand everything but bit by bit I'll be seeing his purposes unfold in my life. I may not like everything about this whole set up but he knows how to work every piece to work to my good. He's more powerful than forces that may try to set limits against me due to matters I only found myself into. My role is to focus on him, obey his word and allow him to fulfill his ultimate plan over this entire set-up I found myself in."

For any of us our resolve ought to be that, whatever our limitations, they cannot hinder God from fulfilling his ultimate plans for our lives. He's the one in charge, not our circumstances. Needless to say that we're in this life not to fulfill our fantasy island desires but to fulfill his preordained will for our lives. It is this preordained plan for our lives that's unstoppable for as long as we keep walking with God.

Our circumstances whether from past or present experiences can roar like Goliath if they want to. But the final choice is on each one of us. Whose report will you believe; the report of circumstances or the report of the Lord in his written word? One is proclaiming doom while the other proclaims hope. One is proclaiming a curse while the other is proclaiming a blessing.

Chapter 12:

Overcoming A Guilty Conscience and Self-Condemnation

What is Guilt?

Guilt is defined as a feeling of responsibility or remorse for some offense, failure, mistake, crime, or wrong, whether real or imagined. It is associated with negative feelings such as shame, remorse, anguish, torment, self-condemnation, self-unforgiveness, self-judgment and in extreme cases, severe depression.

Marks of self-condemnation and guilty feelings

The following are marks of guilty feelings for both real and imaginary guilt. Their intensity may vary from individual to individual. Some signs may also be absent in one person while present in another. It's merely a basic list of signs associated with feelings of guilt. It is adapted from James A. Fowler's article on guilt, "Christ in You Ministries" (ChristInYou.net).

1) Nervousness
2) Depression
3) Defensiveness
4) Suspicion of others
5) Sleeplessness, insomnia
6) Fear, panic attacks
7) Escapism, flight
8) Insecurity
9) Judgmentalism
10) Lack of concentration
11) Shallow friendships
12) Blame others
13) Self-contempt, self-denigration, self-condemnation
14) Addictions, self-destructive behavior
15) Works and performance

Genuine guilt vs false or imaginary guilt

There are two types of guilt:
1) genuine guilt and
2) false or imaginary guilt.

Genuine guilt arises after a real violation of one's moral beliefs. In our case as Christians it arises after a real violation of God's biblical tenets and principles. Imaginary guilt on the other hand, arises from imaginary or illusory violations of one's moral beliefs. The individual actually feels guilty without committing any violation. In the secular professions this type of guilt is considered among categories of mental illness and is also classified as an anxiety disorder. From our Christian perspective they are aspects of a wounded spirit. It is rare to come across committed Christians suffering from imaginary guilt. A rare, or once in a lifetime, experience is no cause for alarm. Certain experiences in life can cause our emotions to go astray.

An example of a rare experience of an imaginary guilt is one I once faced. It lasted about four months. It was way before the Lord revealed principles being shared in this book. I began feeling guilty of wrong decisions a dear person made. The wrong decisions brought more trouble to the individual and for some reason I felt it was my fault. It was so agonizing carrying the blame. My friends were puzzled by this. No matter what they said it made little sense. Some experiences the Lord allows us to go through their entire process before receiving deliverance.

"When you pass through the waters, I will be with you; and when you pass through the rivers, they will not sweep over you. When you walk through the fire, you will not be burned; the flames will not set you ablaze," Isaiah 43:2.

How did I receive deliverance? Through prayer. I used to constantly bring the matters I felt responsible for before the Lord.

Eventually he answered saying I was not responsible for the actions of another individual. And even if I was one prayer was enough to clear me from the debt and receive his forgiveness.

It didn't come from an actual voice of God. If you're waiting to hear an audible voice from God, He speaks or relates to us in different ways and at different times. God spoke to me in a way that I got the truth on the matter and received freedom by knowing the truth. All the guilt, anguish, torment, self-condemnation vanished.

The purpose of guilt from our conscience

Genuine guilt or true guilt is healthy to a certain level. Genuine guilt is the emotional voice response from our conscience that enables us to stay on or get back to a path of behavior consistent with our beliefs and values. When we think or attempt to say or to do something contrary to our conscience a sense of guilt wells up in us condemning us and insisting to do or say the right thing. The Holy Spirit uses the conscience to convict us if we attempt to stray or end up straying from God's word.

Most people have a working conscience. Some people do not have a healthy conscience. The bible speaks of people *"whose consciences have been seared as with a hot iron," 1 Timothy 4: 2.* A person with a seared conscience or burnt conscience does not feel guilty for doing wrong. He cares little about other people's interests and primarily only thinks about his interests.

The conscience becomes seared when inner convictions of right and wrong are rejected on a constant basis that an individual blunts the conscience. It becomes dull or deadened. The conscience grows weaker and more silent in the individual. It becomes ineffectual. The person ends up experiencing little to no guilt for any wrong thoughts, words or actions.

Overcoming unscriptural guilt

The conscience helps us to realize genuine guilt. We have also seen how important and healthy experiencing genuine guilt is.

Beyond the healthy level of genuine guilt is the unhealthy level. This is where an individual feels constantly guilty over past wrongs, failures and sins. Some refer to individuals nursing guilt and self-condemnation over past flaws as having an overactive conscience. An overactive conscience is the opposite of a seared conscience. A seared conscience is a dead conscience whereas an overactive conscience is excessively diligent. It is picky, unforgiving, naggy, and hard to please and constantly brings up the bad past to torment the person. Doesn't this sound like demonic influence?

How does a believer end up succumbing to demonic influence bringing such torment? Unbelievers may have less protection since their sins have not yet been taken by Christ. A believer on the other has redemption through Christ. Why still play the record of the bad past that's been erased in heaven? The main answer lies in the word ego.

Ego from its basic academic definition means the self, me, I, or will part of each one of us. You'll see shortly why we need to use some of this secular academic theory and terminology. As said earlier, there is nothing wrong or sinful about the secular academic world in its non-infiltrated context. It is the matters that contradict or undermine the bible that are a no-no for us.

The ego is a big makeup of an individual's personality, according to the psychodynamic theorists in psychology who assert that personality is composed of three structures:
1. the id (our impulses),
2. the ego (self, me, will),
3. and the superego (our conscience).

The ego wills, chooses and makes decisions based on its perceived inner realities (influences from the id and influences from the superego) and based on its perceived outer realities.

For a believer, the ego is not expected to be willing, choosing and making decisions based on its own nature and faculties. It is expected to operate under the influence of the Holy Spirit and subjection to the statutes of God's word. This is where the problem arises in regard to guilt. The individual is influenced by his/her own inner impulses and perceptions instead of being influenced by the Holy Spirit and by the tenets of God's word.

In fact among Christians the ego is being redefined as an abbreviation for Easing God Out. I believe this a better definition than the complex psychoanalytical term. An individual being influenced by his/her own ego impulses is therefore easing God out of his/her perceptions, decisions and actions. Instead of God being in control the self is. This is natural for a non-believer but unnatural for a Christian.

A believer is expected to naturally allow God to be the one in control - through the Holy Spirit who dwells in us and through his word that is our instruction manual. If a Christian is not he/she is said to be misaligned or in disequilibrium. It's stressful living in a misaligned state. It's also grieving the Holy Spirit. We strive to be well aligned or in equilibrium with God when we're striving to live according to his word. The bible is said to be an abbreviation for Basic Instructions Before Leaving Earth (B.I.B.L.E). It is an instruction manual for our lives.

What does God's word say about our past sins and wrongs?

God's word says volumes on this topic. Even if you're a baby Christian that has just received salvation you know that Jesus was sent to rescue us from paying the penalty of our sins. He is our

Passover Lamb that God sacrificed to pay for our sins, regardless of how bad they may have been. Through Jesus and his work on the cross we receive mercy or forgiveness from God. That is why we have such amazing scriptures like:

- *"Thanks be to God--through Jesus Christ our Lord... Therefore, there is now no condemnation for those who are in Christ Jesus," Romans 7:25; 8:1.*
- *"I write to you, dear children, because your sins have been forgiven on account of his name," 1 John 2:12.*
- *"In him we have redemption through his blood, the forgiveness of sins, in accordance with the riches of God's grace that he lavished on us with all wisdom and understanding," Ephesians 1:7-8.*
- *"He himself bore our sins in his body on the tree, so that we might die to sins and live for righteousness; by his wounds you have been healed," 1 Peter 2:24.*
- *"Therefore, since we have been justified through faith, we have peace with God through our Lord Jesus Christ," Romans 5:1.*
- *"For if, when we were God's enemies, we were reconciled to him through the death of his Son, how much more, having been reconciled, shall we be saved through his life!" Romans 5:10.*
- *"And we know that in all things (good and bad) God works for the good of those who love him, who have been called according to his purpose," Romans 8:28 (emphasis added).*
- *"Come to me, all you who are weary and burdened, and I will give you rest," Matthew 11:28.*
- *"Bless the Lord, O my soul, and forget not all his benefits, who forgives all (not some of) your iniquity, who heals all your diseases," Psalms 103:1-3 (emphasis added)*
- *"Since we have now been justified by his blood, how much more shall we be saved from God's wrath through him!" Romans 5:9.*

- *"Because of the Lord's great love we are not consumed, for his com-passions never fail. They are new every morning; great is your faithfulness ..." Lament. 3: 22-23.*
- *"Blessed is the man whose sin the Lord does not count against him and in whose spirit is no deceit. When I kept silent, my bones wasted away through my groaning all day long. For day and night your hand (of judgment) was heavy upon me; my strength was sapped as in the heat of summer. Then I acknowledged my sin to you and did not cover up my iniquity. I said, "I will confess my transgressions to the Lord"-- and you forgave the guilt of my sin," Psalm 32:1-5 (emphasis added).*
- *"Let us then approach the throne of grace with confidence, so that we may receive mercy and find grace to help us in our time of need," Hebrews 4:16*

A lot of the wonderful scriptures on God's forgiveness were written by Paul in the New Testament. In the Old Testament many were written by David. Guess what these two have in common? They were once murderers.

Paul was instrumental in the stoning of Steven and in terrorizing the early church. David engineered the murder of an innocent man, Uriah, so that he could add Uriah's wife, Bathsheba, to his many other ones. He also had so much blood on his hands from numerous wars he fought throughout his long reign.

Is your past like Paul's, tainted with murder and persecution of Christians? Or is like David's with so much blood, including that of numerous innocent women and children in enemy territories? Your answer is probably, "Absolutely none of the above."

If your past is not as tainted as Paul's or David's then it is not fair on yourself to harbor guilt and self-condemnation. Even if it was as tainted or worse off you'd still be able to receive God's forgiveness. He forgives all, not some of, our iniquities (*Psalms 103:1-3*). Both David and Paul did not allow the iniquity of their past to torment their lives. They moved on by allowing the mercy of God to reign in their lives. They did not ego God out of their lives. After God forgave their iniquities they also proceeded to forgive themselves.

If guilt from past wrongs is still tormenting you it means you're easing God out of your life. You're embracing your own perspective over the matters instead of God's perspective. Overcoming the guilt or healing from guilt will come after you ease God's perspective into your life. Maybe you know about the scriptures on God's mercies but still are unable to let go. It is worth constantly meditating on these scriptures until you feel released from the past wrongs.

By meditating on scriptures I mean reading and pondering the deep meaning of the scriptures in relation to God's will. It's not some blanking out trance and mindless activity. Such activities are called transcendental meditation (TM). They also include mindless repetition of words or mantras. Stay away from such.

Some fasting may be worthwhile. Fasting plays a powerful role in our lives, including spiritual detoxification. Through fasting we're able to walk so closely with God that we become spiritually in tune with him. Through such closeness he reveals garbage we may be carrying. He also enables us to easily cooperate with him in cleaning out this garbage of wrong beliefs, mental strongholds, emotional strongholds, behavioral strongholds, etc.

Thus it's embracing the truth or true perspective on the past from God's word that brings freedom. The key is constantly meditating on scriptures, such as the ones given above, until the scriptures on God's perspective over past wrongs truly become alive in your life.

"Do not let this Book of the Law depart from your mouth; meditate on it day and night, so that you may be careful to do everything written in it. Then you will be prosperous and successful. Have I not commanded you? Be strong and courageous. Do not be terrified; do not be discouraged, for the Lord your God will be with you wherever you go," Joshua 1:8-9.

Once you feel released from the condemnation of the past wrongs it means you have successfully enabled the perspective of God's word to influence your view over past wrongs. It also means you have overcome the demonic influence that was using the past wrongs to bring torment. Satan rejoices when we're down and defeated by circumstances.

The most common experiences that result in unhealthy guilt

The following are the most common experiences that result in unhealthy or unscriptural guilt:

1. People experiencing bereavement,
2. death or injury of others from a car accident or other accident,
3. abortion,
4. divorce (as a child or estranged spouse assuming responsibility),
5. parent dealing with a wayward child,
6. some former military combatants (veterans), or
7. some people once in the occult.

Notice that it's mainly among normal people in society. It's not from among most hardhearted criminals, drug traffickers; human body parts traffickers, child prostitution traffickers, business executives exploiting employees or consumers. Most of such hardhearted people have seared their conscience and thus are unable to have any feelings of guilt. There is still hope for them to return to God and heal their seared conscience.

It is those with a conscience that experience unhealthy guilt from the past. It is my prayer that the biblical info shared in this chapter on overcoming guilt will bring the liberating truth. *"You will know the truth, and the truth will set you free," John 8:32.*

It may be worth acquiring more information from other sources if necessary. There are many ministries, books, and other resources on specific sources of unhealthy guilt. Also, one could fully utilize local library, church and internet sources. For example, on abortion there is a wonderful ministry called Love From Above Inc (LoveFromAboveInc.com). It was founded by Yvonne Florczak-Seeman who had five abortions before she was twenty years old. She suffered years later from devastating emotional consequences until she received salvation. Her salvation was her path to receiving God's deliverance and healing.

Chapter 13:

Deliverance from Demonic Experiences & Manifestations

Spiritual wounds easily mistaken for demon possession

This is only one area of many different areas in a wounded spirit. It is not in the area of demon possession. However, it is easily mistaken for demon possession. It can only be a case of true possession if a person has not yet received salvation. Demonic possession and demonic influence are two different activities in the spirit realm.

Some Christians believe they're demon possessed because they sometimes experience some type of demonic manifestation, such as sensing, seeing, and hearing evil spirit beings. So demons have to be cast out. The biblical truth is that a Christian cannot be demon possessed. The bible is clear here no matter what scriptures some may try to twist to say otherwise.

Being God's children our spirits are sealed as God's own temples. They cannot be defiled by any evil spirits. Thus evil spirits cannot get inside of us in our spiritual makeup. The only access evil spirits have to Christians is from an external position. Such external access is known as demonic influence or demonic interference. Fallen angels can sometimes be given such access to our bodies from an external point that it may seem like they're inside. Remember these are spirits beings that have no limitations to penetrate physical matter.

In relation to our human spiritual and physical makeup the following are the major areas of access among Christians who experience demonic influence or demonic interference:

- Body sensations. These include (real and imagined) feelings of movements in the body, tension, heat flow, and pulsation. Other experiences can include out-of-body experiences.
- Vision perceptions. This includes seeing spirit beings that other people cannot see with their ordinary or human sense of sight.
- Auditory sensing. This is where one's sense of hearing can hear voices of spirit beings that other people cannot hear with their ordinary or human sense of hearing.
- Olfactory Sensing. This is where one's sense of smell can smell odors in an environment that other people cannot smell with their ordinary or human sense of smelling.
- Sensing a presence. This is where an individual sense a spirit being is around. Most times they can also say its hiding but it's around somewhere. The person may say it's watching everybody's movements.

For Christians such demonic manifestations are external types of interference and not internal possession: The above list is by no means exhaustive. It just outlines the major areas of such spiritual manifestation. Some experience only one kind of manifestations. Others experience more than one.

You'll notice that the entire list above consists of spiritual experiences beyond our ordinary or earthly senses. They are supernatural experiences. This is at least where the bible is concerned. The secular world of mental health puts them in the category of psychological disorders. However these are spiritual matters beyond the mind. Many people experiencing such demonic manifestations are actually intelligent and mentally sound. That's why secular remedies fall short. Some trigger-happy deliverance ministers jump to quickly categorize such experiences as aspects of demon possession. So they venture on casting out the demons out of a heaven-destined, God-fearing Christian.

In relation to a Christian the above matters are aspects of demonic influence. Thus the level of access to a believer that demons have to manifest is in this nature is at the level of demonic influence. It is an external type of interference, not an internal one. For Christians it does not graduate to the level of demonic possession.

In a little while I'll cover on tapping into the wrong spirit world as the cause of such manifestations. As God's children we are sealed by the Holy Spirit living inside each of us. It is only if the Holy Spirit were to be grieved enough through repeated and grievous sin that demons could have some room of entry. God forbid that any of us sink to such a level. At such a level one salvation is lost.

Thus for as long as one remains saved his/her spirit can NOT be owned by evil spirits. It cannot be possessed by demons. A Christian's spirit is already owned and occupied by the Holy Spirit. The Holy Spirit cannot dwell or tolerate to live in the same house with an evil spirit. This is the Holy of holies living in us. Let's not insult God by assuming he can coexist with the filthiest and the most evil beings. Each of us is his temple.

However, although we're sealed and thus protected from demonic possession there is demonic influence that we can experience. Everyone goes through demonic influence in some form. God does allow demonic influence up to a different level, during different times, and in different areas among different Christians. Temptation is the most common form of demonic influence. We have the final say on how to respond to demonic influence.

Thus some, for reasons of being able to tap into the spirit realm, are able to experience demonic influence through demonic manifestations outlined above. Remember Paul who received a thorn in the flesh from Satan that brought much pain and discomfort in his life. Was he demon possessed? Absolutely not.

"There was given me a thorn in my flesh, a messenger of Satan, to torment me," 2 Corinthians 12:7.

What causes some people to sense evil spirit beings?

Seeing, smelling, sensing, or hearing demon spirits means a person is able to tap or have access into the spirit realm. The matters that caused this access can be anyone or a combination of matters that open doors to demonic influence. Through any of these doorways an individual may end up being able to sense, see, smell, or hear evil spirit beings that we're not to ordinarily perceive. It may be worth giving examples how any of the four doorways may end up an individual to tap into the spirit world or have access to perceive the evil spirit world.

Through Deception or Ignorance

Falling to deception or falling to ignorance have been put together because it's either one or the other that may result in following false beliefs. For someone to fall into the occult either deception or ignorance led him/her into it.

People involved in the occult and witchcraft are more prone to being opened up to the evil spirit world. This is because occult rituals invoke or call upon evil spirits in the spirit world.

The following is a statement from someone in the occult answering the question: What Can You Expect from Ritual Magic? It is adapted from the Llewellyn Encyclopedia, said to be the most authoritative New Age and Occult encyclopedia.

"These spiritual entities, which are not composed of flesh, always surround you—they are around you even as you read these words—but your dull, material eyes are blind to them. You cannot feel their touch, hear their voices, or see their forms. As you continue the regular practice of the art of magic they will begin to caress your awareness, particularly during the actual rituals.

Yes, spirits do exist. You can prove this to yourself easily enough through the regular practice of ritual. You will find that you have a harder time convincing others of this fact, even as a person with normal sight might find it hard to persuade a man color-blind from birth of the wonderful difference between green and red. Spirits are experienced subjectively, in that someone whose consciousness has been changed by ritual can see them, while another may not see them," (Llewellyn Encyclopedia, "What Can You Expect from Ritual Magic?" by Donald Tyson).

Thus once those who tapped into the wrong spirit world through occult practices have their perceptions open to the wrong spirit world they need God to close their access to this unseen evil realm. God is able to restore their sensory perceptions to only perceive the physical world. The only spiritual realm he leaves open for us is access to him. God is our only spirit being we're biblically permitted to tap into.

Though "tapping into God" may not be a perfect terminology it shows that we have one spirit realm we're permitted to connect with. Our Christian rituals (disciplines) of prayer, fasting, communion, obeying God's word, charitable works, walking in love etc, enable us to effectively connect with God and be led by his Holy Spirit. We never get to see him but we're able to perceive his leadings in our lives in a deeper way; the closer the walk with God the deeper our fellowship with him.

Another form of falling to deception or falling to ignorance is through some false teachings in the body of Christ. Some sincere believers previously involved in false teachings on spiritual warfare that bombard evil spirits can also be prone to perceiving evil spirit beings. The false teachings on spiritual warfare tap into the evil spirit world. The erroneous teachings on spiritual warfare have non-biblical spiritual warfare prayers, deliverance prayers, binding and loosing demons, etc. They all amount to tapping into the wrong spirit world.

Through sin

Occult practices by their nature constitute sinful practices. Thus they're also part of this category. Whether committed knowingly or out of ignorance sin has the same consequences. Sin is basically either deception yielded to or ignorance in application. Apart from occult practices sins that can result in taping in the spirit world include bitterness, anger, unforgiveness or vengeance over past wrongs one innocently experienced as a victim. Culprits or offenders against innocent people are also prone though they may also experience other non-spiritual torment. Others include severe conflicts between a parent and a child, murder or applying erroneous teachings like ones on spiritual warfare that tap into the evil spirit world.

Through storms of life

Some people may find their spiritual faculties opened to perceiving the evil spirit world through any of the previously mentioned storms of life. Sometimes such experiences of perceiving the evil spirit world start from childhood. The child having such manifestations is experiencing something that occurred without his/her input. It is a storm of life. In many cases such a storm on a child may also be an act of demon possession. Thus where it's precisely determined that it constitutes demon possession the child would require demons being cast out.

As you may be aware by now I'm against the trigger happy habit of some deliverance ministers wanting to cast out demons in situations where a person is not even possessed. Thus discernment and scriptural understanding is important. Otherwise it would lead to more problems to a victim who'll keep seeking demons to be cast out of him/her when they're actually operating from an external sphere.

Deliverance and healing from deception and ignorance

These two usually go hand in hand What is required is only repentance for the non-biblical practices, occasional fasting for some, and the truth in God's word being applied. Deliverance follows while healing may not be overnight.

The healing part includes God's work of closing one's spiritual faculties from tapping or having access to the wrong spirit world. For some God's healing their spirit from such ruin may be instant, others a few days, some a few months. It therefore depends on God, the Healer. As a casualty it's important to cooperate with the Healer by walking an upright and prayerful life, applying worthy Christian disciplines.

Deliverance and healing from sin

Deliverance and healing comes through obedience to God's ways and seeking him to close the spiritual faculties that were opened through the sins.

Deliverance and healing from storms of life

There is a solution through Christ no matter what incidences opened one's spiritual faculties to be able to see, hear and experience the evil side of the spirit world. This is more so when it resulted from storms of life. Seeking God to close the spiritual faculties from perceiving the evil spirit world is the key. God is the Healer. It's worth focusing on him to complete his healing work of one's spirit.

How do we receive deliverance from demonic manifestations?

In God's eyes the cure is the same for all afflictions. However we have made it seem like some afflictions need special deliverance because of their severity. Believers being told they need special deliverance end up moving from one "deliverance ministry" to another, sometimes coming out with worse afflictions than before.

Firstly, a believer needs to be open to searching for doorways in his/her life that may have given access to experiencing and seeing in the spirit world. After finding matters that were root causes of demonic visions, voices and perceptions a believer needs to deal with these areas to close the legal doorways. No demons need to be cast out of a born again Christian. The problem is with external influence, not with internal influence. Whatever the cause God is able to bring deliverance to a believer.

If an individual can sense, see, or hear demon manifestations it does not mean the demons have gained more power over him/her. They are as powerless as the ones not seen. They can scream and say "we're watching you," but that does not mean they have any power over you.

Seeking God's intervention

A believer's prayer and appeal to God is to seek God to close his/her spiritual eyes and faculties from seeing, hearing and sensing these spirit beings. He'll need to continue seeking the Lord's deliverance and healing from not being able to see, hear and sense these spirit beings. When the Lord brings this victory it means that his faculties have been restored to the level we are ordinarily made of - not being able to see, neither hear nor sense evil spirits.

This will not mean their demonic influence attempts have ended. It will only mean their power to inflict underserved spiritual torment from their external influence has ended. They can no longer be seen, heard or sensed so they can make all the noise they wish but a person is shielded from seeing into the spirit realm. If we all could ordinarily see into the spirit realm it wouldn't be a pleasant experience constantly watching ugly beings.

It'd be nice to sometimes see God's angels conquering the demons though. Our faith would be energized, knowing that those who're with us are more than those against us. But that would be walking by sight (what we see) instead of faith (trusting God and his word). Maybe that's why God doesn't ORDINARILY allow it, given that we're beings created with senses to perceive matters in the physical or earthly realm.

God made us primarily for the natural realm. This is the reason why we have bodies and can ordinarily see each other and interact with one another. He then kept the spirit realm to his domain. That's why we do not ordinarily see the billions (if not trillions) of spirit beings (good and bad) busy at work in the spirit realm. On rare occasions he does allow some people to see into the spirit realm. For example God allowed Elisha's servant to see the vast angels protecting them when he was afraid of human enemy forces (*2 Kings 6:16-17*).

Thus a born again Christian who is able to experience manifestations of spiritual beings on a constant basis ought to continue seeking God to close his/her senses from perceiving the spirit realm. Seeking God to close one's senses from perceiving the spirit realm is more important in relation to the ugly manifestations, which are demonic manifestations.

There is no need to run to a so called "deliverance ministry" that casts demons out of Christians. Such a Christian is experiencing aspects of demonic influence not demonic possession. You don't have to run to ministries that bring more bondage instead of deliverance. Such ministries are unscriptural preoccupied with casting out demons that have already been evicted by the Holy Spirit in believers' lives. Being Christ-centered instead of demon-centered is the key to deliverance and healing.

Standing in faith & obedience throughout the healing process

Standing in faith and obedience to God throughout healing process is important. No need to speak to spirit beings. In fact please do not speak to them. Some believers I have counseled have said speaking to them makes them leave for a while. But they still come back.

There is no need to keep going in circles. The demons end up playing hide and seek. They claim to be inside a believer (an aspect of demonic possession), when they are actually operating from outside (an aspect of demonic influence). Playing their game keeps them working through the doorways.

There is no scriptural example where someone was speaking to spirit beings except those demon possessed. You or your born again loved one cannot be demon possessed. A born again believer cannot be Holy Spirit possessed and demon possessed at the same time. Your experiences are a result of demonic influence and not demonic possession.

Speaking to evil spirits in thin air is not scriptural. Yes Jesus spoke to the devil in the wilderness but look at its context. Did the prophets do it? No. Did the disciples do it? No. Did the apostles do it? No. Neither should we.

Speaking to evil spirits only invites their presence; it is calling them forth or summoning them into a sphere that your spirit and senses are able to recognize and interact with them. It is tapping into the spirit world, the wrong spirit world. Once your spirit and senses are able to recognize and interact with them the experiences are nothing but ugly.

Some experiences may seem like one is demon possessed yet it is mere demonic influence. Don't rush to categorize some experiences as demonic possession, when in fact they are actually from demonic influence. Some deliverance ministries rush to cast out evil spirits that are not even in a person. Because this is not what's required, a person who has non-existent demons cast out ends up never experiencing any deliverance. He/she feels more confused wondering why the demons have not gone. This is because the demons were never inside. The individual may begin feeling more discouraged and defeated. He may assume there could be something wrong with him for having demons not being able to be cast out. What is actually wrong is the deliverance ministries that label nearly every problem as an aspect of demonic possession. It is the deliverance ministry, not a believer in the wrong.

Sometimes the intensity of demonic influence increases after going to these supposed deliverance ministries. Their intensity increases not from an internal influence, but from an external influence. The demons taunt the individual that they will never get out. He/she is their home. Yet those are only lies to continue focusing on their non-existent internal presence.

As long as one focuses on the wrong causes there will never be a solution. God forbid. Sometimes out of desperation a believer may try all kinds of remedies to get rid of their harassment. Some begin to bind and cast them out, to plead the blood of Jesus against them, to plead the blood of Jesus upon themselves, rebuking the demons, seeking deliverance ministers to cast demons out, getting into spiritual warfare prayers or deliverance prayers that directly confront the demons, etc.

Unfortunately most of these assumed remedies are the very avenues that demons are invited into a realm where one's spirit and senses are able to experience them. So believers or deliverance ministries who practice them only invite more demonic activity.

Under no circumstance are we to speak to demons in cases of demonic influence. We're to speak to God only in the spirit world. Ignore the evil spirits and get into a prayer session, speaking to God who will eventually close your eyes from seeing evil spirits in the spirit world. Prayer combined with fasting also helps. Until God completely closes your access into the spirit world your focus should be on him not the evil spirits being seen or heard. In his time God will bring the required covering to your spiritual eyes and senses. You'll be like the rest of us who are covered from seeing and hearing these evil beings.

Continue doing your part of seeking God's intervention and walking an upright life. If you're interceding for someone facing such spiritual attacks your challenge is ensuring you're a clean vessel for the Lord to effectively use. Our obedient lives are weapons of righteousness that enable our prayers not to be hindered. This is indirect spiritual warfare. *"Submit to God and be at peace with him... You will pray to him, and he will hear you... He will deliver even the one who is not innocent, who will be delivered through the cleanness of your hands," Job 22: 21, 27, 30.*

Praise and worship music is another weapon against spiritual attacks. It can help in facilitating the healing process. Through his continued disobedience the Lord allowed a tormenting spirit to come upon Saul. *"Now the Spirit of the Lord had departed from Saul, and an evil spirit from the Lord tormented him," 1 Samuel 16:14.*

One of his servants knew a remedy to this. *"See, an evil spirit from God is tormenting you. Let our lord command his servants here to search for someone who can play the harp. He will play when the evil spirit from God comes upon you, and you will feel better,"* 1 Samuel 16:15-16. Another servant recommended David who was at this time hardly known.

The music from David proved to be good medicine for Saul. "Whenever the spirit from God came upon Saul, David would take his harp and play. Then relief would come to Saul; he would feel better, and the evil spirit would leave him," 1 Samuel 16:23.

Chapter 14:

Deliverance & Healing from the Occult

Deliverance from Witchcraft & Satanism

While I have zero personal experience in such areas deliverance and healing principles are the same for all problems whether resulting from false doctrines in the body of Christ, from false religions, from past abuse, from sin, or from involvement in the occult, etc.

At least this is the case when applying biblical principles, not psychiatry, medicine or other non-Christian approaches. Some deliverance ministries have complicated and polluted biblical deliverance principles with rituals, constant "spiritual medications" such as binding and loosing demons, etc. These have only brought more demonic attacks on individuals. What matters most is the area where deliverance is required -spiritual, social, material or physical.

Some involvement in the occult may have been minor yet resulted in strange experiences and demonic attacks. If people that where deeply entrenched in occultism can be delivered and healed; how much more a one time or casual encounter? What brought their deliverance and healing is nothing but their willingness to follow through the biblical principles God has given us.

Please stick with God's plan for your salvation and see what he'll do in your life. Avoid deliverance ministries that try to bind and loose demons in their attempts of casting out demons. It is true that extreme involvement in the occult can result in demonic possession. Yet it's also true that deliverance from demonic possession comes through accepting Jesus Christ as personal Lord and Savior. When Christ is invited one's spirit is reborn into a new nature that is under the ownership and possession of a new Spirit, the Holy Spirit.

The deliverance from demon possession is instant. Healing from past possession is what can prove to be challenging for some. Because some individuals' faculties remain open to seeing, hearing, and experiencing the activities of these spirit beings that we ordinarily are not designed to see their tormenting attempts can persist after deliverance.

If the new believer, who is now God's child, is not wise he/she may believe the spirits still own or possess him. The fact is that they do not own or possess him. They no longer live inside him. Their attempts and fights to return may seem like demonic possession yet it is an aspect of demonic influence, not possession, it is from an external position. This is an aspect of demonic influence, which everyone is liable to.

The only difference is that the individual's faculties remain open to seeing, hearing, and experiencing the activities. His prayer and appeal to God is to seek God to close his spiritual eyes and faculties from seeing, hearing and sensing these spirit beings. He'll need to continue seeking the Lord's deliverance and healing from not being able to see, hear and sense these spirit beings. When the Lord brings this victory it means that his faculties have been restored to the level we are ordinarily made; not being able to see, hear nor sense evil spirits.

This will not mean their demonic influence attempts have ended. It will only mean their power to inflict undeserved spiritual torment from their external influence has ended. They can no longer be seen, heard or sensed so they can make all the noise they wish but the individual is shielded from access into the spirit realm. If we all could ordinarily have access into the spirit realm it wouldn't be a pleasant experience.

You may find Jeff Hershberger's book, "From Darkness to Light" helpful. Harshbarger is a former Satanist now in Christ and is the director of Refuge Ministries International (www.refugeministries.cc). By the way, there were no demons cast out of Harshbarger when he was delivered from Satanism. Being Christ-centered instead of demon-centered is the key to deliverance and healing.

Other Titles Available From VIP Ink Publishing!

Hard Questions About

GOD

By Only A. Guy

Hard Questions About

Jesus

By Only A. Guy

Hard Questions About

The Holy Spirit

International Bestseller

By Only A. Guy

Hard Questions About

Salvation

International Bestseller

By Only A. Guy

they are real.

ROBERT CONNERS

THE GREAT DECEPTION:
Why Are They Here?

Stanley Simmons

COMING SOON AUGUST 27, 2013

A DEEPER CHRISTIAN LIFE

DR. NANCY HAYES

www.ingramcontent.com/pod-product-compliance
Lightning Source LLC
Chambersburg PA
CBHW061724020426
42331CB00006B/1074